Principles of War

By Archduke Charles
von Hapsburg

Translated by
Daniel I. Radakovich

NIMBLE BOOKS LLC

Nimble Books LLC

1521 Martha Avenue

Ann Arbor, MI, USA 48103

http://www.NimbleBooks.com

wfz@nimblebooks.com

+1.734-330-2593

Copyright 2009 by Daniel I. Radakovich

Version 1.0; last saved 2010-06-09.

Printed in the United States of America

ISBN-13: 978-1-934840-97-9

Contents

FOREWORD

It is always something of a puzzle how to enlist the interest of the hapless reader in a foreword . For if the author has anything of value to say, it is more apt to be ignored or lost there than if properly placed in the concert of the body of the work; and if it is of no or little value, then why bother with it at all? Most of the time forewords seem to be devoted to dedications anyway. But there are times when the presence of a foreword is a useful thing, and that is when the work itself may be wrongly considered mere ephemera of historical curiosity value at best. Such is the case with this one, originally titled *Gründsätze der Höhenkriegskünst* by the Napoleonic era's Archduke Charles von Hapsburg of Austria ... herein translated into English as "Principles of War" for simplicity's sake. A more literal translation could be "Fundamentals for the Higher Warcraft."

In the field of military history, it is all too common to refer to ancient tomes of strategy and tactics for no better reason than idle curiosity, to picture to the author-and, if he is competent, his reader- the movements and actions that were undertaken by the sides in a particular battle or campaign to help them get to a finer understanding of what happened in the milieu of the period. All well and good, but esoteric surely for those whose interest goes beyond reconstructing the past. The work presented here is not one of generalizations for strategic thought or stratagems of war like those perused by any overly enamored of potential business applications. The world has recently seen practically every major writer on military strategy essayed to fit into preconceived molds for that sort of writer trying to validate all sorts of things the originator could not have possibly contemplated their work would be used to justify or illuminate. That does not mean that these forward-looking applications of past insight are without some value, but again clearly the value resides in whether or not the person reading it is concerned with the applied subject.

This work, which, although coming out under the auspices of the Archduke Charles was in effect a committee effort, it was an attempt to reassess what had gone wrong in recent years, to delineate what had gone right, and in what [in the appended chapter about the French wars] might need still to be re-evaluated. We see a period of transition in a major failed organization, which is seeking to requalify and revalidate its own tradition in new circumstances, by identifying earlier ways in which the perceived traditional wisdom had become warped or perverted out of the norm, and to recreate the past successes by a return to a "fundamentals" *weltaanschaung*. The book was created in the middle of the most critical period in the existence of that state, after some five successive failed campaigns that had seen it stripped of its most ancient title of Holy Roman Empire, and losing approximately a third of its territory and most of its prestige along the way. In the entirety of the catastrophe only one leader had come even close to an even match with the newly constituted but ancient foe, France, and that was Archduke Charles. He had beaten several of France's marshals and had performed creditably against their "first teams" of Bonaparte and Moreau. Indeed, a few years after composing this book, Charles was one of the few to win a battle against Napoleon at the height of his career. (His victory came at the place called by the French "Essling" but by Austrians "Aspern," so the rest of the world often calls it by a hyphenated conjunction "Aspern-Essling.") Months later Charles was decisively beaten at Wagram, but it was a "damned close-run thing" as a certain British leader of the period might have said.

Withal this is a "loser's book." Its possession did not make the possessors able to win against superior forces, as reputedly was the result of Frederick the Great's *Instructions*-though the mere mystery of the rumor of the *Instructions* was a more valuable asset than their actual possession, just as the supposed keys to his success were mistakenly taken to be continuous parade ground drills. *Le Grande Frédérique* was above all a pragmatist, and often ignored what he himself had written in his earlier tome ... as indeed was Charles. Why, then, is there any use at all in looking at *The Principles of War?*

Well, for one thing, the winner of those conflicts-Napoleon- did not write a "how to" book.. The methods and procedures of Napoleonic France are not as clear-cut as the historian would like. Many writers from Jomini and Clausewitz to the lesser-known lights that Napoleon critiqued on St. Helena and the American distillers like Winfield Scott, Henry Halleck and Hardee, attempted to create something like a "recipe book" of how the armies of *L'empereur* achieved their successes. Even the best of these authors, who had fullest access to the several drill manuals and tactical tomes and volumes and campaign overviews, kept coming up with inconsistencies and confusion.

Principles of War is a primer for generals. It is perhaps difficult to believe that one would get to such a high command level without already knowing the contents, but the peculiarities of the multi-lingual multi-national forces of the Austrian realm made this remedial work not only desirable but a necessity. Of all the challenges in competition through teamwork, be they war, sport or business, the chief difficulty is to get everyone on the same page. A common melody sets the tune from which any riffs or variations can be undertaken.

Principles of War is meant to give the basics of the art of war in the same way that an art book talks about how to draw a line to perspective. As a primer, it never attained the higher repute at the time of the more theoretical geometrically-nuanced proofs of Jomini or the Kant-like philosophical musings of Clausewitz on the nature of war itself. However, unlike the German sage's *The Art of War*, the *Principles* was at least completed. It enjoyed a fair vogue in the period immediately after the Napoleonic era, coming out in Germanic and French versions, one copy of which is known to have travelled with a British general[Charles Napier] in campaigns upon the Indian subcontinent. The Austrian losses at Solerfino in 1859 and Koniggrätz-Sadowa in 1866, where presumably they followed these precepts, most likely led to the demise and disuse of *Principles*...though Benedek disdained to follow several of Charles' caveats on how to march and prepare for battle in his preliminary campaign.

En fine, what is the utility of perusing this work? *Principles?* It is an example of how in a field of intense and deadly competition, in the middle of crisis, an attempt to find an answer was found. It may have been imperfect. It may not have been the best answer. But it was *an* answer, and it served well enough to take the Austrian army through the next eight years of war (1807-15) with more creditable results and less friction and ineptitude than theretofore. It is "one of life's little victories" over entropy, mistake, error and all the ills the Fall of Man lays us heirs to. Whether the causative factor be termed Satan or Murphy its goal is the same, and it must always be fought.

SHORT BIOGRAPHY

Archduke Charles von Hapsburg's full name in German was Karl Ludwig Johann Josef Lorenz, Erzeherzog von Österreich und Herzog von Teschen. He was born in Florence, Italy on September 5th, 1771 and died on April 30th, 1847 in Vienna, Austria. He had a notable career as an army commander in the French Revolutionary and ensuing Napoleonic Wars, beginning as a brigade commander at 21, achieving army command at 25, defeating commanders as diverse as Jourdan, Moreau, Bonaparte, Masséna, and Ney, and though at Teining Bernadotte gave him a check, the future Swede was forced to withdraw later. Charles also had his own share of defeats as well, but he was clearly on their level in strategic and tactical leadership. He was diagnosed with epilepsy at an early age, although it was at most an exceedingly mild form and may well have been another nervous disorder. There is no reliable record of this condition having any adverse effects upon his generalship, though as may be understood it at times was blamed for his few failures. Ill health of another sort is credited with his departure from the military in 1798, but it may have been politically engendered rather than physiologically. He was reportedly short, around 5' in height, which makes him one of the few people Napoleon topped in that area ["Boney" was 5' 6 1/2"—the traditional 5'2" is a mistransliteration of French pre-metric measurement into English standard]. After Wagram Charles was retired from command—presumably because he was against the Napoleonic alliance politically, more practically his disgust at losing Wagram had caused him to "lose it" threatening decimation of the ranks[killing one in ten], etc.—except for a short period when he commanded the fortress of Mainz after the Hundred Days campaign in 1815. Had Napoleon managed to defeat Blücher and Wellington the odds are that Schwarzenberg and Barclay de Tolly would have met him next, not the old sparring partner in Italy and Bavaria the Archduke Charles. Charles married later in 1815 and had several children, one of whom, Archduke Albrecht, was regarded as an excellent general in his own right, commanding in chief in Venetia against the Italians in 1866. Later Charles inherited the duchy of Saxe-Teschen from his childless aunt's husband; they had fostered him as a young man, as Charles' father the future Kaiser und könig Leopold had a large brood and took pity on his sibling's childless state.

Figure 1. Archduke Charles. (Heinrich Schmidt
with engraving for the colorized mezzotint
by Valentine Green, 1799)

METHODOLOGY OF THE TRANSLATION

In making this translation I used chiefly the 1848 French translation of the work, as it was done during the putative author's lifetime and was capable of correction thereby, double-checking it first against a reprint of the original German, then a copy of the original. The translator has tried to keep the flavor of the original, with its somewhat stilted phraseology, and in cases something like double or triple negatives result, which might lead to some confusion. But any errors are the translator's own mistakes, and he begs pardon in advance for any that might exist.. For the notes and comments, of course these are the translator's own opinions, and must be taken with a grain of salt, as anyone's comments should be. Back in the 1980s, the original translated rough manuscript was hand-circulated among a number of Napoleonic scholars, chiefly through the interested contributing subscribers to the Napoleonic review *Empires, Eagles, and Lions*. It is dedicated to two absent friends from Indiana who believed in it, Dr. Gunther Rothenberg, formerly of Purdue University, and Jim Mitchell, formerly of the *Seven Years' War Journal* publication. *Requiescat in pacem, fratres.*

CHAPTER 1

1. General Considerations on War

War is the greatest evil that can happen to a state or nation. The principal need of a sovereign or a general-in-chief thus will be to call up from the beginning of the war all disposable forces, and to employ them in such a way that the war lasts as shortly as possible and ends quickly in the most favorable manner.

The object of all war must be an advantageous peace, because only an advantageous peace lasts, and it is only a lasting peace that can, by making nations happy, accomplish the ends of governments.

Decisive blows alone can accomplish this great end. The principal art of a general thus consists of appreciating and weighing the instant and the point where such decisive blows can be struck with the greatest probability of a happy result.

Such a decisive blow cannot be struck upon such a point unless one is superior in forces.

Most of the time, armies posted against each other are proportionally equally strong in number of troops; the decisive point is therefore unique; because one can only unite a superior number of troops upon a single point.

These principles which are in the nature of war, and which alone lead to decisive results, give the true definition of the art of war: It consists of the art of uniting and employing a superior number of troops upon a decisive point.

All generals should take this principle as their guide, in great operations as in secondary operations, in offensive war as in defensive war, in a word, in all possible circumstances.

2. On the Arms Composing the Armies

To put this principle into execution, armies are the most essential means.

They consist of infantry, cavalry, and artillery, which are subdivided into infantry of the line and light infantry, cavalry of the line and light cavalry, and artillery of the line and light artillery.

The nature of these diverse arms and that of the terrain determines their employment.

As no terrain exists where it cannot operate, the infantry will be found, except in entirely flat country, to be the uniquely preponderant arm, and that is why it must form the most numerous part of armies.

Line infantry forms the elite of infantry; it determines the victory by how it energetically defends closed posts and positions, and by how it attacks the enemy in his own with courage and resolution, etc., while the light infantry guarantees it from surprise, surrounds it like a fence, and harrasses the enemy, because its nature permits it to be employed and to act in a scattered manner.

The particular quality of horse determines principally the way in which one employs the cavalry. As its exclusive property consists of the arrangement and rapidity of movements, and of the attack, it cannot be so advantageously used [elsewhere] as upon a flat terrain.

It covers the wings and flanks of the infantry, it often re-establishes lost combats, it throws itself upon the flanks of the enemy infantry and thus determines the victory, etc.

The same principles by which we have determined the different method of employing line infantry and light infantry, should be observed in the employ of the diverse types of cavalry.

Light cavalry covers the flanks of line cavalry, forms the greatest part of avant-gardes and rear-guards, as well as detachments flanking the columns, and, seeing its celerity and lightness, is preferentially employed in surprises, in excursions, in a word, in partisan warfare.

Artillery finds itself, by its two types, in the same condition as the two arms mentioned above.

Heavy artillery serves in the attack or defense of positions, light artillery in rapid movements and for accompanying light troops.

In the employ of all these arms one should never lose sight of the fact that there is only one decisive point, on the defensive as well as on the offensive, and that in consequence one cannot produce important results, decisive, save by the greatest possible concentration of all forces upon that point.

3. On Diverse Types of War

There are two types of War:

1st.

War of attack.

2nd.

War of defense.

A decisive superiority in both the quantity and quality of troops, or great advantages in the nature of the terrain which will be in the theater of war (advantages that can even be products of art, like a line of fortresses, etc.), authorize a general to conduct war offensively, just as the lack of all that constrains his adversary to bear a defensive war.

At all regards the first is the most advantageous, and conducts most rapidly to the end. All its operations are all the more easy as the enemy is forced to direct his own after those of the army acting offensively.

Nothing can authorize a state to wage a defensive war, if it is not an inevitable necessity, without the prompt perspective, to see eventually the certain possibility that, by reason of changes in its political relations, or by a decisive blow struck by the general-in-chief, it should pass from the defensive to the offensive.

4. Of the Plan of Operations

In conceiving a plan of operations, one should never lose sight of the principal end of war, obtaining as quickly as possible an advantageous peace. In consequence all must tend to constrain the enemy to this peace as promptly as possible by decisive blows.

It is not until after procuring a certain knowledge of the means of the enemy, as well as the country in which one is going to operate, that one can project an exact plan of operations.

Here is a capital rule as good in offensive war as in defensive war: with the principal force never take a line of operations or a position so that the enemy is nearer than us to our lines of communications, our magazines, our convoys, etc.

A general who neglects that rule will often find, after the happiest events, he is in the necessity of abandoning all the advantages obtained, and to make a shameful and strongly disadvantageous retreat, without having lost a battle.

5. On Offensive War

In offensive war, the principal task of a general must be to seek to profit as soon as possible from the advantages that put him in the position of having the power of conducting a war of attack, to foil from the beginning the intentions of the enemy by decisive operations and to put him in such a state that he can never regain the superiority.

To that end he must open the campaign with all the forces united upon the decisive point, and, on the contrary, not occupy all the other frontiers of the state save with the absolutely necessary number of troops, for covering these provinces against enemy incursions and to prevent the enemy from raising for his army means to pursue the war.

The country destined to serve as the theater of war could be open, defended by fortresses, broken, or mountainous.

In each of these cases, the point upon which he must penetrate and operate with all his forces, is that which leads in the shortest and most prompt manner to the interior of the country, without our incurring danger for our communications by this.

Nothing should engage a general to depart from this principle. His first effort thus tends to open the campaign by a decisive battle, and to constrain the enemy to accept it. Until that he will measure each of his steps and will only advance with the greatest circumspection. But once the battle is won, he will penetrate rapidly and resolutely to profit from the victory and not give the enemy any repose.

In open terrain, where superiority of force can principally decide things , that operation will find few difficulties.

A lot more prudence and an exact knowledge of terrain and of all the auxiliary means that the enemy can employ to halt our progress are needed, when the operation takes place in a broken or mountainous terrain, but even in these cases the principle of operating upon the decisive point with all his forces stays unalterable. Only by making an exact reconnaissance of the country, by assuring one's rear and the flanks by expressly sent detachments and by taking all precautions, can one prevent the danger of being surprised by an overlooked movement of the enemy, or being constrained to inaction, if not a retreat, by deceptions there where the terrain offers him some advantage.

6. On Defensive war

The Principles of defensive war derive in great part from those of offensive war.

The principal tasks of the defensive are to gain time, to defend and to guarantee against the enterprises of the enemy the country it possesses.

One fulfills the first of these conditions, in avoiding all action which will be decisive for the enemy, and the second in keeping united upon the decisive point for the conquest of the country all disposable forces, and in joining able maneuvers to the choice of good positions.

A great number of generals adopt the erroneous opinion that one should cover a country by establishing long cordons, by the occupation of each of the points of the frontier. As a result of which they sacrifice the defense of a whole country to the defense of a village or a small zone, which puts all advantages between the hands of the enemy as soon as he penetrates with his united forces upon a single point.

As victory upon the most advantageous point of a frontier can alone lead to ulterior conquests, one cannot deflect this evil unless stopping the enemy with force on the decisive point, and in carrying this out, to guarantee remaining frontiers from incursions, to employ small detached corps.

Should the enemy try to penetrate upon several points and thus let escape the advantage of his superiority; then one can, from the point where all the troops are united, fall successively upon each of his isolated corps, beating one after the other and thus giving the war a whole new direction.

In defensive war in mountainous country, one still cannot avoid the essential principle of concentrating forces upon the decisive point. He must not be induced into error by the specious advantage that offers us the defense of all the passes and all the defiles giving access to a country.

The mountain range one must defend, is that with only one sole principal passage, or where it encloses several practicable routes by which the enemy can penetrate to our magazines, our communications, etc.

In the first case one places at that passage the bulk of our forces, and one will chose the point of defense there or at the pass that presents the most natural difficulties for the enemy, difficulties that art may perhaps make greater still.

The avant-garde will occupy the exit from the mountain to the plain, less for defending that point than to be instructed of the movements of the enemy and to profit from them as well, either by a return to the offensive, or by all other manners, from the faults that he may commit.

If the mountain to be defended presents several passages equally advantageous to the enemy, the defensive there offers greater difficulties, except when valleys crossing it lead ordinarily to such means of entry, having between them several communications.

If the roads which can serve the enemy must concentrate upon that point of the bulk of the army, one should not occupy the passes save with light troops that one supports by several detachments pushed forwards.

If the enemy attacks one of these passages; then all these outposts and detachments will retire upon the army not to be exposed to the danger of being cut off from the principal body of troops, of their communications and their magazines, by the enemy who can advance if he has been fortunate upon one point.

The situation of things and the nature of the terrain then shall indicate to the general-in-chief, whether he can await the enemy at the point where the army is placed, and if he should retain the defensive, or go to encounter and attack him. In mountain warfare this last part is thus the preferable, above all when one has the advantage of better knowing the terrain and the countryside.

A mountain range in which go parallel roads, which almost never converge, if it is not at least unique to the heart of the country, and has not by this any liaison between them, is very rare; one cannot conveniently defend it save by uniting the army in one of these defiles, as much as possible in that which has the closest proximity to the enemy line of communications, and in occupying other defiles by simple detachments. The enemy thus will find himself unable to enterprise anything important without risking the greatest danger for his lines of communication, until he has beaten or at least repulsed the principal army, and our need will be met if we constrain him to operate against the point where we can make the greatest resistance to him.

The defensive will be almost impossible against a superiority that allows the enemy not only to oppose a superior number of troops to our army, but also to operate with energy upon another point.

7. On Fortresses

Fortresses situated upon the frontiers of warring powers change all conditions of war.

Fortresses are destined either to the simple defense of a country, or to serve to support offensive operations. The task of the defensive is to gain time; that consideration must never be lost sight of in the choice of emplacing fortresses to defend a country. They will thus be placed in such a manner that the enemy cannot easily leave them behind him without risking all for his communications and his convoys, and that by this he is obliged to leave in his rear a considerable force to observe them, blockade them, or besiege them, which will weaken his army and make it incapable of an ulterior offensive.

This end cannot be attained in an open country, save by placing fortresses at the principal entries to the country, as well as at points where great roads go to the interior and where roads of communication cross them; or even upon navigable rivers, and principally upon those which flow perpendicularly in a country, and which can in consequence serve as communications and support to the two parties, etc., and by giving these fortresses an enclosure such that they can contain a strong garrison and to be also abundantly provided with all necessary for their defense.

But in the case where fortresses must serve uniquely as the defense of an isolated point, as for example a defile in mountains, etc., one should make them small. As the end of their establishment must often be attained by very little means, it is necessary here to keep to the most necessary works. Nature will indicate the point upon which one constructs them, that is to say the point where they will most easily fulfill their destiny.

For fortresses destined to serve as supports for offensive operations it is necessary to have regard principally to the points upon which an offensive war could and should be conducted against the enemy; in consequence at the principal entries to his country, and upon communications with the same country.

They should be able to contain important magazines, and be situated in such a way that in case of contrary events they cover the retreat of the army, and impede the progress of the enemy. They should be by this of a considerable size.

There is a third sort of fortress, which is less for the defense of frontiers than for the security and retention of the whole country. These fortresses should be placed in the interior of provinces and are properly called "places d'armes." Their purpose consists of conserving supplies of all sorts for the training and equipment of armies, receiving beaten troops and improving their organization and their armament, and offering a rallying place for military forces still existing in the provinces. But such fortresses must have a great enclosure: they must be upon central points, where the routes unite from the exterior to the interior, and from where communications extend to the countries in the rear; or even "à cheval" upon navigable rivers, they must assure communication of the two banks.

The rapport of one state with another, and the measure of the influence it wishes to have on its neighbors or that its neighbors wish to have on it, determines the necessity and the importance of fortified points for the conservation of its proper independence.

The system of fortifications is thus based upon the disposable military forces of the nation; because what use are fortresses, that bleed by their extent an important part of the troops destined to fight in the open field, and which lack the possibility of remedying that diminution of active armies without stripping themselves?

Places d'armes contribute a lot to the interior force of a state, as they act upon the whole. But by that reason, and because of their importance by their size and their position, their number must be strongly restrained. Often a sole *place d'armes* suffices for a state. On the contrary it is necessary that for covering the frontiers, with very few exceptions, to have many fortresses. Their situation and their force determine thus the allure of operations as much for the offensive as for the defensive.

The siege of a fortress deprives the army levying it, and that destined to cover it, of an important part of their troops. Thus it should not be enterprised save if a great disproportion exists between our forces and those of the enemy. In consequence a campaign will never be opened by a siege, before a decisive combat has been gained over the enemy; except in the sole case where he finds himself in so evil a situation, that one can by a preliminary reconnoitering assure oneself that one will have the time to take the fortress, before the other will be in a state to try anything to help it.

In mountain warfare the positions of strong places at the principal entries, or on the necessary passages, indicate those which one should besiege and those which need only be blockaded: in open country, on the contrary, it is necessary to know if it is covered by one or several fortresses, and if they are large or small.

A small fortress that does not precisely cover the principal entry to a country, deserves little attention, for it can be observed or blocked by a weak detached corps.

But if the fortress is on the contrary large enough to contain a considerable garrison, magazines, etc., and if by this' it not only guarantees the country from the enemy, but if it could also, in the case of a happy event, offer him the means to help him pass from the defensive to the offensive against us, then it is inevitable to besiege it, and with the principal army one cannot take any more important step forwards, before it has been conquered.

When there are several small fortresses, it is necessary to take the most important, to isolate the others; and, as soon as the one takes the most advantageously situated, the others become prevented from being a whole, they can be blockaded with a few troops and find themselves in the impossibility of enterprising anything against our communications, then only one can push forward with the principal body of the army.

If one or several ranks of fortresses cover the enemy frontier; then he assures himself of those that can harm us most in case of misfortune, which are found upon our lines of communications, at principal entries to countries etc. One should open the campaign with their siege and preferably by the siege of the fortress which is found situated at the principal entry to our land, and as much as possible by the siege of the most considerable. It is not until after its conquest that one can penetrate with confidence into the interior of the enemy country, as soon as our frontiers are perfectly covered, as soon as our magazines, our convoys are assured; as soon as we have created a base from which we can advance without fear, and in case of contrary events, not only make an advantageous retreat, but also conserve an honorable defensive.

Always, even in the greatest prosperity, a general should not lose sight of the fact that he must not try an enterprise that in case of failure would become more dangerous than his happy success will have procured him advantages.

8. On Winter Campaigns

As winter campaigns often have as an inevitable consequence the ruin of the armies, one should not undertake them save in the pressing necessity of defending oneself. Or, if the special advantages that the winter campaigns permit compensate for this disadvantage: for example, when the enemy army is so beaten that one can flatter oneself, by continuing the campaign into winter, with destroying him entirely; with making some conquests, to penetrate so far into enemy country to constrain him to peace; when one possesses intelligence in the country, or knows of events of such nature that one cannot take advantage of them save if one utilizes them without losing time; as for example a cold which, in freezing watercourses, suppresses all the obstacles that they oppose to marches; or when the enemy has so ineptly taken his winter quarters that one can attack them advantageously, take his quarters, disperse and obliterate his army.

In similar campaigns or enterprises, the general-in-chief should do all that is possible to sustain the troops by all that can alleviate and render more supportable in anything the fatigues and maladies that are inseparable from winter expeditions: by that he will obtain the great advantage of preventing at least in part the ruin of the army.

Figure 2. A contemporary portrait of Archduke
   Charles (1812).[1]

---

[1] http://commons.wikimedia.org/wiki/File:Karl_Austria_Teschen_
1771_1847_ color.jpg

CHAPTER 2

1. On the Emplacement of Magazines

The regions where one must place magazines containing all necessary objects to an army are determined following the general plan, of the design that the operations will take, and one should not ever enterprise one thing before the needs of the army are entirely assured.

The principal line of operations thus will be that of the magazines, and the army will cover them by its movements.

The principal magazines should be placed behind rivers, or else at the points where the majority of roads converge and lead along the lines of operations of the army, and as much as possible be in fortresses, or in places that can be held against a coup-de-main. One will echelon[deploy]small supplementary magazines midway between these principal magazines and the army. Finally magazines of consumption will be established in the vicinity of the army, and as their emplacement will often change following the operations of the army, these last magazines will not contain provisions for more than 8 or 10 days.

Fortresses, even those which are the most exposed, ought to be provided with all that is necessary for their defense from the beginning of each campaign, not only for all the time during which they could sustain a siege, but at least one-third more in food.

If only enough is provided for the time during which they could sustain a siege, then the most important reason for their creation will in great part fall. The enemy who can in effect, by this hypothesis, take it as rapidly by a blockade as by a regular siege, will not be forced to undertake that siege which would have as a final result the considerable weakening of his active army, and will put it out of a state of enterprising ulterior operations.

2. Of Marches

As much as a general should be lively and decisive on the day of battle, so much should he be cautious and circumspect in the projection and execution of his marches.

The purpose of the march determines the order of march, and the nature of the terrain the number of columns in which the army should march, as well as the arms that should compose each of these columns.

In every case, he should march in as many columns as he can form, without their being so weak that they do not in themselves have almost any independence. The distance between these columns will be that which they need to mutually support each other and deploy commodiously.

The force and the composition of the avant-garde or the rear guard will be determined by the position in which one finds oneself vis-à-vis the enemy; they will always be composed of light troops. While one has the unique design of forming a chain of outposts before the army, as well as to cover the movements which one makes, and to amuse or stop the enemy precisely long enough so that the general-in-chief, instructed of the position or the approach of that enemy, will gain the necessary time to make his dispositions with the army, then one should not push the avant-garde in front or leave the rear guard behind any more than what is necessary to accomplish their tasks, and in this case these troops of the outposts should advance with the army, and depending upon the circumstances, be placed on the wings, within villages or broken terrain, before the front, etc.

Whenever an army finds itself in a position such that, where it is obliged to make a march such that the heights, the defiles, etc., situated between it and the avant-garde cannot be occupied by either of them, because they are situated neither on the principal position, nor along the chain of advanced posts, and while meanwhile their occupation and their defense is inevitably necessary for halting the enemy, and covering the retreat of the advanced posts, etc.; in this case, one will detach there troops of the line which, after having accomplished the task of their mission, should return to the army without waiting to be engaged in a serious combat and destroyed by the enemy approaching them.

The armies can execute three sorts of marches, in front, to the rear, and to the side or by the flank.

If the march in front takes place against an enemy, each column will be preceded by an avant-garde of which the composition wil be determined by the task one undertakes by making that march, by the proximity of the enemy and the nature of the terrain one must cross.

In a retreat the rear guard will be composed in the same manner; the column against which it is most likely that the enemy can enterprise undertake something with advantage, should be the strongest and contain the best troops.

In the march by the flank, the heads and the tails of the columns are the flanks of the lines of battle one will form, and by this will be the weakest parts. It is why the avant-garde will be separated between the front and rear of the columns, principally of the column finding itself closest to the enemy; the rear guard covers, in this case, the march of the columns, and also their ulterior advance, in that when it halts in the position where it should arrive, it then advances a little against the enemy, and creates by this the possibility to the columns of freely continuing to march behind them.

Flanking patrols and small detachments garnish the columns only on the side of the enemy, from which there is at least little to fear, because in case of need one can in several minutes face front against the enemy by a conversion of battalions.

In open terrain, the order of march is not subjected to any difficulty. Only one should never neglect the precept of marching in such a way, that one is always able to advance rapidly, and to put oneself in order of battle upon the side from which the enemy could come.

The march of the artillery train and of the baggage should always be made, as much as possible, upon the most advantageous road and the farthest from the enemy, and one will have need of placing them in the column in a manner by which they will find themselves sufficiently covered. In case of a retreat, one will leave them, with foresight, in the rear, with a certain lead on the enemy.

In broken terrain, one cannot know how to march with over much prudence and circumspection, when one finds oneself in the proximity of the enemy. All the country will first be scouted by the light troops; each defile, before which one will not pass it, will be strongly enough occupied so that one can defend it, and that the passage of the columns can be protected against an enemy attack.

But if, despite all precautions taken, the enemy anyhow surprises the avant-garde, crushes it and is advancing so rapidly upon the heads of our columns in march that we no longer have time to arrange the army in ordinary order of battle, then nothing is left to do than to deploy the battalions at the heads of the columns.

That done, one can, if a favorable terrain furnishes the occasion, either attack the enemy without reservation, or halt him until the point where these battalions are deployed, until the army will have gained the time necessary to put itself into order of battle behind them.

If the enemy wipes out these troops by his superiority, we will meanwhile have attained our principal task; the army will be delivered from the imminence of its loss, and the general-in-chief, by the sole fact that he will have gained time, will perhaps have acquired the possibility, either by taking a good position, or by beating his enemy by wise maneuvers, or finally, if he has need to fight in retreat, of having the power of continuing that retreat.

3. On Positions, of their Defense and their Attack

One cannot call good a position save that upon which an army finds itself in a state of perfectly accomplishing its task that is proposed in the plan of the general-in-chief, and which guarantees at the same time to that army the certainty of being able to accept battle with advantage, in the case where the enemy attacks it.

In offensive war, it will thus always be upon our principal line of operations, in defensive war upon that which the enemy should take for advancing; or if the nature of the terrain, the fortresses, etc. favor the general, it will be on the flank of the adversary, and at the point where the general can operate against the communications of the advancing enemy, thus gaining time and preventing his adversary from penetrating further, as long as he occupies that position; meanwhile he should never occupy such a position when he could by it prejudice his true line of communications.

The principal properties of a good position are to offer sure support for the two wings, (impenetrable to the enemy), of having free communications with the front, to guarantee an assured retreat by several good roads, and to be preceded in front by a terrain that opposes difficulties to the enemy, at the same time as it assures us a free employ of our arms, and which is dominated and enfiladed in all its points by the position.

As to what concerns this last point, one can divide positions into two types.

1st.

Positions where nothing is really necessary but defending the space upon which the troops are placed. These can, at a distance of one-and-a-half cannon shots before the front, not be sufficiently covered to oppose all possible difficulties to the enemy.

2nd.

Positions which are but destined to favor the tactics of the army, and from which one has the intention to maneuver against the advancing enemy, as for example positions which one takes for a quarter of an hour, a half hour behind an important defile, to entice the enemy to pass it with his army, and then to attack as soon as a part of his troops have traversed it.

These positions must be open upon their front or on the flanks, upon which is found the point against which one will put oneself into movement for the poser of maneuvering freely, especially when one possesses a cavalry superior in number and in quality.

Positions for the defense of rivers, or of a stretch of country which is open or provided with several openings ending at the same place, are for the most part of this sort: similar dispositions are found above all at the points where the principal routes and the defiles meet.

In general one chooses positions upon heights, because from there one can better see around oneself, and so the enemy suffers difficulties in climbing them. These heights should be crowned by infantry destined to occupy them, in such a way that the troops found formed there follow the configuration affected by the terrain.

The wings and the most pronounced salients before its front, are the most decisive points of each position, these last because by their salients they better flank by their fire the front of the position, as well as the terrain situated in front, and as they by this much augment the difficulty of each attack, as long as one has not got possession of them.

The wings, on the contrary, are decisive, because only being protected by the fire of a small part of the position, they offer to the enemy the greatest facility for an attack the results of which might be extremely disadvantageous, because if he succeeds, the enemy will find himself thus on the flank of the whole position, and that without subsequent resistance he will take in flank all the troops found posted there.

Thus one occupies these wings very strongly with troops and with artillery. This last will always be placed in battery, because the fire of several cannon concentrated upon the same point is the only kind that produces a powerful effect.

Cavalry will not be placed save upon terrain upon which it can act, that is to say on the plains which are found within the position or upon the wings. But several detachments of this arm could be posted here and there behind the infantry that occupies the front of the position, either for making sorties upon the enemy when he is on the point of attacking, or when the fire of the position has already occasioned to him some disorder, etc.

As the attack is the duty of the cavalry, one will place it always at some distance behind the point upon which it should act.

The second line will be posted behind the first, as near as necessary to support it, and finally the reserve will be placed in a third line, either in the middle, or behind the most important point.

A general should never occupy a position, or undertake the least enterprise, without having a reserve which, in all unfortunate events will assure him a retreat, and which can give a good turn to a lost combat, or achieve a victory.

In the defense of positions the reserve should have above all a great part of the cavalry, because it will be principally employed in attacking the enemy, who will have obtained over us some advantages, and will strip him of each of these advantages. It is necessary that the reserve can move rapidly above all for attacking. Rapidity thus should be an essential quality for troops that form a reserve.

In war cases are often presented where a general is constrained to occupy positions that lack one or several essential properties.

Abatis, inundations, entrenchments, the occupation of forts, the opening of communications, etc., are the proper auxiliary means to remedy their faults in many cases. Meanwhile, if these defects depend upon the nature of the terrain, one cannot remedy this great inconvenience save by the method of forming the troops, or even he should never take such positions, whatever advantage they seem to otherwise offer; such are, for example, the following:

1st.

A position good before its front, but upon the rear of which one finds an important defile.

2nd.

A position that offers so little depth that one cannot place more than one line of troops upon it.

Among the most disadvantageous positions are ranked in preference those of which the two wings are not sufficiently supported, or which stretch into the plain, even those which have a single wing supported, because the enemy who attacks an army posted in a similar position with the greatest advantage upon its uncovered flank, will fling it back upon the support of the other flank, which could be a river, a swamp, or all other analageous localities, and could thus make it perish entirely.

The end for which we force ourselves to support our wings, is that we wish to make them unattackable, because they are the weakest parts. But if, by our formation alone, we lift from the enemy the possibility of falling on a wing, we are equally assured, for each case where the nature of the position does not guarantee a sufficient support. To that regard, the formation in echelons offers all possible advantages, as, following exigencies and the nature of the terrain, two, three, or several battalions will be placed in echelon behind the exposed wing, because they there mutually support each other's flanks and are within range of support. The enemy will be thrust into the impossibility of taking the wing of the army in flank, because in this case its own will be exposed to these troops placed in echelons. He can no longer attempt to outflank these echelons by a march because he will in doing so open to his enemy the road of his retreat, his line of communications, and will give him the time, by a flank march, to go with his army to take him in front and likewise in flank; in short, the end of covering and assuring the wing will be completely attained.

A similar case presents itself when both wings lack a sufficient support, or where one of them goes into the plain where it should be covered by cavalry formed in echelons.

There are an infinite number of cases of each type. Each position demands another formation, other dispositions.

It is the sign of a wise general to employ intelligently the principal general rules of the art of war, and to adapt them easily to different circumstances and diverse situations.

There are two means of forcing an enemy to abandon a position: either by attacking and throwing him out of it, which is the most sure when one has a decisive superiority both in the number and the quality of the troops, and is the preferable in the case of a badly chosen position by the adversary; or by prying him out of it by maneuvering. One employs this last method when one cannot count with certitude upon the happy result of an attack, or when one wishes to once more defer a decisive combat, for fatiguing the enemy by movements, to put him into a disadvantageous situation, and to better assure himself of the prospect of a fortunate result, etc.

This end will be attained by some marches upon the points where one menaces his line of communication, from where one can even cut it either with the army, or with flying corps or bodies of partisans, by some menaces or some movements against places the defense of which is so important that he will be thus constrained to abandon his position, etc.

In the attack of a position one should principally take the weakest points, or points which are so decisive that an attack upon all other points is impossible or at least dangerous, as long as one has not mastered it.

Among the first points are ranked in preference wings when they are not well supported, and above all salients, which cannot be defended by the fire of the position; among the last points one finds fortified posts, heights which protect by their fire the front of the position, and smite the flanks of each troop that wishes to pass in front to attack the position upon another point; posts which are found near the road which we have the intention of taking to effectuate our retreat in the case of a repulsed attack, and which flank this road, etc.

In the attack itself, the principle of uniting upon the decisive point all disposable force, and never to try an attack there here if our communications and our road of retreat are not entirely assured, should serve as principal guide. To this last regard, one should even frequently enterprise from preference the attack upon the difficult point, rather than exposing oneself, in attacking a point a bit more advantageous, with the danger of not having an assured retreat, and, in case the attack fails, with the danger of seeing the enemy upon our communications.

The best method of attack is the echelon order, because all the forces thus find themselves united against one point, the lines support each other in echelons, the flanks themselves are covered when they haven't already a *point d'appui* in the terrain, and one or two wings of the army rest so far to the rear or are refused in such a manner that it is impossible for the enemy to turn them by a movement or a thrust of his cavalry, and to take us in flank, and that these can be employed, in case of misfortune, for covering and assuring the retreat. The elite of the cavalry goes after the attacking wing, when the terrain permits, or joins itself to the reserve body.

As soon as the attack is decided, the army will be put in march in as many columns as possible. The columns should be closed and near enough to one another for their mutual support, all the while conserving enough space between them to be able to form and deploy.

When the columns approach the outposts, the avant-garde, which one will reinforce depending on circumstances by a small body of line infantry, marches before the army, at a distance of over a quarter of an hour, to keep our design hidden from the enemy as long as possible, and having as well enough time to surmount, before the arrival of the columns, all the resistance that the enemy's outposts can make.

The avant-garde repulses the outposts of the enemy, occupies the points the possession of which can cover and facilitate our deployment and our attack, and which are indispensable to us in case of a retreat, such as defiles, bridges, villages, heights, woods, etc., then develops in front of the enemy position a chain of skirmishers of light troops, and also makes, when it is judged necessary, (reinforced then by line troops), a false attack and some demonstrations upon the points of the enemy position against which the attack will not be directed. In a word, the commander of the avant-garde should employ all to hide from the enemy the design of his general, and to induce him to error in that regard.

When the columns arrive in the proximity of the enemy position, one deploys oneself outside of cannon shot; some battalions in the first line, in the rear a second line outflanking the first, then a third line, or at least some battalions behind the wings of the second; finally the reserve body, a part of the cavalry with this corps, and the greatest part in echelons upon the wings, if the terrain permits.

If the attack of the enemy position is not very difficult, one should then advance rapidly against it following the formation. If on the contrary the enemy has a lot of artillery upon the point that should be attacked, if it is fortified, etc., then one should, following the formation, advance a little, put in battery as many artillery pieces as possible before the first line and in other favorable emplacements, and unite the liveliest fire against the point of attack, then, when this fire has sufficiently harassed, weakened, and perhaps put the enemy into disorder, march to the attack.

If the attack succeeds, in this case one should rally as promptly as possible the troops that the action has without doubt put into a little disorder, before pursuing the attack against a second line, or against the reserves which the enemy may already have prepared, or even maintain oneself upon the conquered terrain, by which one abandons the pursuit and the achievement of victory to the cavalry, supported by as much infantry as the terrain allows.

But if the attack fails, and if the general-in-chief cannot foresee with any certitude of success, either in augmentation of effort or in making the reserve advance, then one begins the retreat. Under the protection of the refused wing or the reserve, and in flat country under the protection of all the cavalry, the repulsed troops will form anew, occupy the most advantageously situated points for covering the retreat, and retire either from post to post or in checkerboard fashion, until the night, or the army arriving at a tenable position, puts an end to the pursuit by the enemy.

As in the attack upon the enemy's position, the forces should be concentrated on one point, it follows that in case of unhappy events, the retreat itself is found subject to many less difficulties than when the troops are dispersed.

When an attack should be executed by the combination of several columns coming from different points or countries, it is necessary that these columns are not too separated from each other. Finally, one should enterprise [such] attacks as rarely as possible.

The junction of columns can never be calculated so exactly, that obstacles encountered during the march on the terrain, and which can even be occasioned by hot weather, will not halt one or the other of these columns, will not slow its arrival, and will not in doing so cause the whole project to fail.

Among other things, if the enemy takes another position during our march, and the columns are too distant from one another, the commander has neither the time, nor the means of changing the disposition of his columns rapidly enough so that they can act against the new enemy position, before that new enemy position has caused us hann.

Finally, if the army, promptly warned of the division of our forces, falls with his whole army upon one of our columns, one courts the danger that not only that column will be entirely destroyed before it is possible to support it, but that all the columns, attacked one after the other by the enemy, will suffer the same result. Maneuver is much easier for the enemy when he here operates from a central point.

When the general-in-chief has his forces concentrated and his columns in range of one another, there can rarely present an occurrence, or be effectuated a movement of the enemy, against which he cannot immediately take the most convenient dispositions, and guarantee himself from all danger.

In mountain positions, all is borne generally by combats of posts and light troops combats.

The defense of valleys and the defense of mountains are so intimately tied to one another, that when the infantry is dislodged from a mountain, the body of troops that occupies the valley can no longer stay there, and if this last corps is repulsed, the infantry posted upon the mountain has to retire not to see itself cut off from the road of retreat and all the convoys.

The uniquely great advantage that the attacker possesses over the defender consists of this: that, as generally each great mountain is cut by a lot of roads and valleys which do not have between them any junction, or at least when they haven't one situated at the heart of the country, and which by this leads all onto the principal point of the defensive, as well as on the lines of communication, the defender must then divide himself to close similar passages, during which the attacker has only the need to occupy several between them to observe them, and that he can by this throw himself upon one of these with superior forces.

This consideration makes a defensive almost impossible in a mountain where the passages are not defended by independent forts.

In the attack of a mountain position, the principal body of troops, consisting of infantry accompanied by a little artillery and a small detachment of cavalry. will be formed in column in the valley. Then the light troops, supported by a little infantry, will be pushed in front in the mountains situated to the right and left, to purge them before all of the presence of the enemy, after which one can advance in the valley. As soon as this end has been attained, a part of our troops, pushing into the mountains, pursues those of the enemy, while the other part attacks the heights situated to the right and left of his position, or even occupy them if the enemy has abandoned them already, and our column then advances in the valley.

The enemy position and the terrain alone can determine if one should begin by deploying to attack the enemy after having crowned them, or if one should surely and simply attack his position in column.

When the attack does not succeed, the retreat should be effectuated as prudently as possible, and with the greatest circumspection, after which the body of troops posted on the mountain and those placed in the valley will always keep hand-in-hand, to the end that the precipitation of one of these two corps does not procure the enemy the possibility of cutting off the other from retreating and perhaps even to force it to lay down its arms.

To that regard, a general, even after the loss of a battle, should find enough resources in the numerous difficulties the terrain of a mountainous country offers.

The rules which we are going to give for the attack in a mountainous country allow themselves in great part to be deduced from those to be employed in a broken country, where the walls, hedges, ditches, etc. take the place of mountains, only with that difference that the hand of man can in part suppress these last difficulties, as they have none of the inherent difficulties of those mountains.

4. Of Entrenchments

In mountainous or very cut up country, entrenchments can contribute for something in the defense of positions, because they close the defiles by which the enemy inevitably should pass to act offensively.

On the contrary, for positions in open country, entrenchments are shown at times more of a nuisance than useful, because they serve the enemy as visible points against which he directs and concentrates the fire of his artillery, because they show him which points we consider as the most important, and because of which in the maneuvers of troops and artillery, they are very often embarrassing for us, etc. Finally, experience teaches us that an entrenchment resolutely attacked almost never resists the assault of the enemy.

A prudent general thus will carry out the entrenchment of points in his position which the enemy cannot avoid attacking when he attacks the position; he will not utilize, for the rest, entrenchments save to fool the enemy.

5. Defense and Passage of Rivers

In the defense of rivers, as nature indicates the places where crossings are possible, it follows that entrenchments can have, in this case, usefulness for covering from the fire of the enemy the cannon of the batteries that it is necessary to rest, to flank the crossing area. These areas are those where the bank on which one finds oneself dominates the bank of the enemy, or the bank is concave upon the side of the enemy, or a particular current of water, or isles, etc. favors the crossing, and principally the construction of a bridge.

Crossings can be enterprised by two methods, either by force or by surprise.

One adopts the first method, uniquely when the terrain in the vicinity determined for the passage will favor such an enterprise, that by taking along a numerous artillery, superior to that of the enemy, one can purge the opposite bank of all his troops, cross first in boats with some troops under the protection of these batteries, take position and throw a bridge across, then defile the whole army across that bridge, make it advance, and then put one's hand to solidly installing the bridge and to the construction of a bridgehead.

A crossing by surprise can be enterprised with less advantages of terrain, but it requires the most absolute secrecy, and will not ordinarily succeed save when the enemy posts along the bank are negligent, and when the stream is not too wide, or if a special current of water goes very rapidly, and virtually pulls the troop-laden boats from the point of embarkation to the enemy bank.

It is impossible and very dangerous to defend a river with an army by occupying its banks and each point of passage.

If the enemy succeeds, in effect, in crossing at one point with his army - and that will always happen when a river offers some points of passage - that chain will find itself broken without the power of uniting quickly enough, during which the enemy utilizes and rapidly pursues the advantage that he is going to obtain: which to him has become so easy, that on no part will one be in a state to stop him.

In the defense of a river, it is necessary thus principally to judge what will be, in case of an offensive, the true principal line of operations of the enemy, and upon which point he should cross and advance to find himself upon the same line.

It is necessary to unite on that line the principal army, at the same time as a chain of light troops occupies with the necessary artillery the whole bank of the stream, or to observe it at least with uninterrupted patrols, posts of small flying corps detached vis-à-vis the areas of crossing, and there raising batteries to halt the enemy, if he dares to make a tentative attempt.

The principal army will be, as much as possible, placed upon a point where numerous routes cross, from which it can move itself freely and without obstacle, and at a sufficient distance from the bridge so that it does not carry the danger of being surprised, or being led into error by some demonstration, and so it will not be put into movement before one knows the true intention of the enemy, either by his dispositions, or by the very manner in which he attacks the outposts; then, advancing with all its forces against the principal point of attack, one can assail the enemy who could not have passed but a portion of his troops, and throw him back to the other side of the river.

If one thus obtains the victory, the intention that one has in making that attack will not be completely fulfilled; it is still necessary to create by this the possibility of the defensive-offensive shift.

The attacking portion in this case does not even court any danger for its retreat, as it finds itself along the principal line of operations of the enemy, and by this upon that which it should take in last resort to retire; while the detachments and bodies of light troops placed along the bank, will always have the time to retire before the enemy can gain any serious advantage over them.

If the enemy traverses the river upon another point than that point presumed, then he will find himself, after having effectuated his passage, either nearer or farther than us from our line of communications. In the first case there remains nothing else to do for a wise general save to put all in motion to get ahead of the enemy by forced marches; in the second case there is nothing better to do than to profit from the fault that the enemy committed in choosing a defective point for his operation; he will let them thus advance for several marches into the interior of the country, and can then direct himself with his army against their flanks, or take their communications from the rear, to constrain them promptly to a disadvantageous retreat.

6. Of Winter Quarters and Cantonments

The manner in which it is necessary to post armies in winter quarters is derived from the intention for which one takes them. This intention consists of procuring the army the occasion of reposing itself and rebuilding itself, and to place at the same time these quarters in such a way that by their establishment one conserves the points which can cover the countries in possession of which one finds oneself at the end of a campaign.

Security against enemy attacks, and the possibility that the troops can concentrate upon the principal point of the chosen line of defense, before the enemy has penetrated it, these are in consequence the principal qualities of winter quarters.

When one can take them covered by important defiles, such as watercourses, mountains, etc., they offer the great advantage of being more secure, and of permitting by this the troops to occupy a much more spread¬out space.

Before winter quarters one places a chain of outposts, behind which, above all upon the principal points upon which the enemy can advance, one posts, depending on circumstances and in preference in open country, some important support bodies in narrow cantonment, and as this means must make the troops suffer too much, one relieves them from time to time; this is named the cordon of outposts.

At the outposts, as well as at the emplacements of corps destined to support the outposts, it is necessary to use all. means to make access difficult for the enemy.

Behind the position, one determines the points upon which the army should concentrate in time of danger in case there is need to assemble; points which it is necessary to choose following the operations that the enemy can enterprise.

One places thus the army in its winter quarters, in taking above all into consideration that the all the parts of that army should find themselves equally distant from the principal position, that is to say from that which is found upon the principal line of operations, following which the troops, in case of alarms occurring, can attain that position in about the same space of time; the cavalry, which can make much stronger marches, will thus be cantonned as closely as possible, without in all cases the men losing something relative to the repose and well-being of which they have need, and without the country being too crowded.

Finally in the fixation of the placement of the outposts and their supports, as well as the positions which should be chosen for the assembly of the army, and the fixation of the quarters themselves, it is necessary always to adopt as a principal duty to calculate all exactly enough to be sure that the outposts and their supports will be in a state to halt the enemy long enough so that he cannot attain the position destined for the army before the majority at least of that army has arrived.

The same principles that should direct a general in regard to winter quarters are also those which he should take for rules when during the campaign the army will find itself in the case of cantonning. This case presents itself, it is true, rarely; but an unforeseen evil time, a circumstance which often prevents a general from profiting from the success he has obtained, or the necessity of procuring the army the means of reposing itself and rebuilding itself, etc., can determine them there, while unforeseen movements of that enemy will not force it to sudden counter-movements. As they are not taken up save for a short time, cantonments of this sort have over winter quarters the advantage that one can concentrate troops in them in a much greater number.

It is equally necessary to not lose sight of the fact that here the principal rule is to post the troops in the way that all the troops can be united upon the decisive point of the line of operations in the least possible time.

Only an ignorant general, to whom the principles of the science of war are not familiar, who will not know nor discern the decisive point, nor will recognize its importance, divides his forces either on the offensive or on the defensive.

In offensive war, from great operations to attacks of positions and posts, he is deprived by this method of acting of all the advantages which can authorize him to make an attack, and creates for the enemy the possibility of throwing himself with all his forces and by this with superiority against his bodies of isolated troops and to beat them one after the other, without him being able to resist him, making fall not only the combinations of his plan by this, but allowing his whole army to be destroyed in detail.

In defensive war, in which one finds oneself most of the time constrained by the superiority of the adversary, one cannot assuredly do anything more contrary to the end than to render that superiority even more decisive, in putting oneself at the same time in a state of not being able to make in a single sector even a mediocre resistance.

Figure 3. A sketch by Johann-Baptist Pflug.[2]

---

[2] Pflug, Johann-Baptist, Bildnis von Erzherzog Karl von Österreich, Bild, Biberach an der Riß, Städtische Sammlungen, Braith-Mali-Museum. http://commons.wikimedia.org/wiki/File:Karl_von_Österreich-Teschen.jpg

CHAPTER 3

1. On the Escort of Convoys

When the operations are directed following just principles, the magazines are placed conformable to the march of these operations; it is thus only rarely that the case will be presented of where the convoys have need of a special escort, because they are ordinarily sufficiently covered by the position of the army.

While a general-in-chief can be in the necessity of detaching a particular body for protecting a convoy, the force of this body should be calculated following the greatness of the danger, its composition following the nature of the terrain in the crossing of which it must march until its reunion with the army.

The principal quality which is necessary to a general commanding such a corps is foresight.

If, on the one hand, it is important that he attain his end as quickly as possible, it is meanwhile even more important that he attains it securely, because often the issue of the whole campaign could depend upon the exact arrival of a convoy to an army.

The countryside in which such a convoy must march, will probably be known with exactitude, be gone over and scouted in all of its aspects, and never should a march be undertaken without one having obtained admissible and reassuring reports in this regard.

46

During the march, the column of the convoy will be surrounded by a chain of light troops who will keep themselves at a convenient distance before it, for being able to make known to it in time each approach of enemy troops, beyond that chain one pushes in front and as far as possible some parties of cavalry, to obtain news.

The bulk of the corps destined to escort the convoy will be preferably concentrated upon the point where the greatest danger is found exposed. I say concentrated, because it is equally necessary not to neglect the principle so certain that one cannot attain an end save by the unification of one's forces. But one will employ upon the other points small detachments of troops.

Has one something to fear for the head of the convoy? In this case the general precedes it with his escorting corps, and occupies each advantageous position upon which he can resist the enemy, or halt him, as well as each defile.

If, following the configuration of the terrain, the occupation of a second position a bit further is necessary, then it will retire as soon as the head of the column arrives, and goes to deploy itself: if not, it suffices to throw in front of the convoy a simple avant-garde, and to conserve with the principal corps of troops the first position until the bulk of the transport is found there. Then, one halts with the whole column of vehicles, one advances anew with the troops of the escort before the head of that column; one reunites the small detachments which are sent back from being of the tail and flanks of the convoy and one employs them to occupy the defile in the rear or the first position until the whole convoy has passed beyond.

The same rules also serve for the case where a danger menaces a convoy from the rear; with this difference that one should never then abandon an advantageous position, before the tail of the transport has passed and gone beyond a certain distance.

The escort of a convoy will find itself exposed to greater difficulties when the convoy is attacked by the flank, principally in broken terrain and when it is necessary to pass several defiles.

In covering a convoy with his force a general should have as his principal rule, to always occupy the point by which the enemy has the greatest facility and advantage of attacking; to take that position, before the head of the convoy has attained that height, to occupy it until the whole convoy is found to have gone beyond a certain distance, and of not employing beside the columns ought save weak avant-garde and rearguards.

In an entirely open country, the corps destined to cover the flanks marches opposite the middle of the column of wagons; an avant-garde precedes and a rearguard follows.

The principles which should serve as guide to the general for covering a convoy during its march should be equally observed when he is required to establish it on a position in case of an imminent enemy attack. The corps will be concentrated upon the most menaced point, there will take the most advantageous position possible, and will be placed there in such a manner that it will be impossible for the enemy to place himself upon a more advanced point and to attack the convoy before the arrival of the escort. The wagons, on the contrary, that compose the convoy, will park upon the most convenient spots in several sections, each section will also be as closed as possible and forming a "masse." Munitions wagons will form the masse farthest from the enemy, the horses will be unharnessed and placed in the least exposed neighborhoods.

This method of parking the wagons is very preferable to that employed until the present of forming them in barricades of wagons, because it demands less time to execute, takes less space and demands fewer troops for their defense.

The troops which cover the convoy, should they be forced to recoil before the enemy, then shall place themselves among or behind the masses of wagons, by which they will be much better protected than by a barricade of wagons. And if they should fight in retreat, they have a greater probability of being able to deliver several of these sections, or at least the horses, while they bum the wagons left behind.

It is not necessary to make a stay save where one can post oneself advantageously. In the number of these neighborhoods are those points upon which the wagons can park in several sections, concentrated as much as possible, to diminish also, as much as possible, the perimeter to defend. In the attack upon a convoy one cannot chose a more propitious moment than that where it has begun to become engaged in a long defile, because one can worry it from all sides, it and the troops surrounding it, and above all halting it by an attack upon the tail, as well as looking to separate the tail from head and center. One should principally make the strongest demonstrations against the point upon which the general who commands the convoy has taken his measures, and where he waits to be attacked, and during this time to enterprise the principal attack upon another point, as much as possible upon the flank of the center of the column.

The faults of the enemy general, and above all the default of foresight, can often offer the occasion to make advantageous attacks against convoys. It is necessary to profit from them with the greatest activity and the greatest secrecy, for not leaving to the enemy the time to attenuate his faults, or to be instructed of the advance of the project that one forms, and by this be able to make preparations for opposing them.

2. On Demonstrations

One names "demonstrations" any movements destined to mislead the enemy as to our intentions. For attaining this end., they should be such that one can promise oneself his enemy will be duped by them, and that is why they should not indicate anything but some intentions presenting a real degree of military realism. As their end is uniquely the induction of the enemy into error, in consequence facilitating the execution of a plan, but not of deciding it, it is not necessary to consider these save as an accessory; also they should never weaken or diminish the means necessary to the execution of the principal project to the point of exposing it, that the success of a demonstration is only the realism and depends upon the manner in which the enemy appreciates it, while, on the contrary, the hope of the success in a decisive enterprise should base itself upon an exact estimation.

One distinguishes three types of demonstrations:

1st.

Great demonstrations, which are destined to induce the enemy to error on our whole plan, by the indication of the allure of future operations, either at the beginning, or during the campaign, and which must be executed by the means of disseminating some troops in quarters or cantonments, by the concentration, the emplacement and the movements of an army, by the establishment of magazines, by the repair of routes, entrenchments, etc.

2nd.

Demonstrations which have for their object less important ends, and which in consequence cannot be executed by ought save a small corps, as for example to attract by means of menaces or real incursions the attention of the enemy upon some country, to carry him to weaken his army by some detachments, etc.

3rd.

Demonstrations before or during a combat, of which the principal end is to mislead the enemy as to the point where he should be attacked, and upon the manner in which one has resolved to execute the attack.

These demonstrations consist of simulated attacks with the avant-garde or some detached corps upon one or several points, as well as in the formation of the army, either in the order of battle, or in columns, against the points which one has decided not to attack, but from which one can, always keeping covered by the terrain, or by the avant-garde, or by false attacks, throwing oneself promptly upon that where one must have the decisive attack, etc.

In all situations in which a general may find himself, there is among all the operations that he can enterprise but one real operation, the most conformable to the end, the most corresponding to circumstances. The demonstrations can on the contrary be as numerous as can be produced by the combinations of human intelligence as long as they obscure the truth. It is always necessary to prefer those which indicate the most realistic operation. One executes them most easily when a favorable position or the superiority of forces allow taking the offensive, and they will be then very dangerous for the adversary who, in the case of the defensive, is obliged to adjust his movements to those of his enemy.

So as not to curry the danger of being fooled by means of demonstrations, a general will first calculate with justice which is, of all the possible operations that the enemy can undertake, the one which responds best to his end. It is against this operation of the enemy that one should before all guarantee oneself, prepare oneself, post oneself, direct all one's movements, and then he will never fail. Where the enemy acts according to true principles, and in this case one will be prepared in advance, or where he avoids them, thus committing a fault, and a wise general will know how to put it to profit.

But how will the general distinguish, in the last case, if his enemy is not merely making demonstrations, or if he has really adopted a defective plan, and if he has made ill-combined movements? How will he avoid the danger of falling, without risking anything, into the inconvenience of not being able to utilize the fault of the adversary during enough time so that that adversary could repair them?

This military problem, one of the most difficult of the art of war, merits being analyzed.

The demonstrations of the enemy can consist either in simple armaments, or in real operations such as movements, marches, displacements of the army or corps, etc.

It is necessary to consider the first with attention, but a general should never abandon a point that different considerations place upon the veritable line of operations, or weaken himself there, to prevent his adversary upon a less important point, even when the enemy concentrates some troops upon the last point.

As to the second case, it is not more necessary here to make any decision before one has obtained most certain information upon the marches of the enemy, when one even should lose a little time, because that loss will be always easier to compensate, and will be less of a nuisance than to separate oneself from an important line of operations by the premature abandonment of a decisive position.

Has one the certitude that the enemy has concentrated his army and begun his operations upon a point where one has not prepared, and is this point away from the position of the army? Then one must once more wait, and perhaps, either by a position, or by movements against the flanks or rear of the enemy, prevent one's adversary from penetrating further, and forcing him to discontinue the operation rather than risk, even in the most unfavorable case, something for his retreat. If the enemy finds himself, on the contrary, so near that one courts the danger of being cut off from the line of communications by a rapid movement of the adverse troops, then it is necessary, depending upon the proportion of forces, either to attack the enemy briskly, or begin a retreat to avoid a disadvantageous combat. But one should never make one of these movements when one is not certain that the enemy has a serious operation for his end, and that he really approaches some point from which he can attain our line of communication before us. Otherwise, he may only have as his end the drawing out of us without fighting from the position we occupy, and so, by nothing save a demonstration made in the proximity of that position, he creates in all cases the possibility of occupying by a rapid movement this position abandoned by us, before we can install ourselves there anew.

But if we conserve our position as long as possible, his whole plan will fail, and the enemy is thus constrained either to change the demonstration begun to a real operation, or to approach us to attack us: by this we will in all cases have gained some time to profit from the mistakes of the adversary, or to avoid a combat.

The same principles that a general should observe in operations, not to be induced into error by some demonstrations, can, on a lesser level, serve him as guide on a day of battle.

Here once more is only one essential point; here once more, in an attack or in a movement against another, the enemy may have no other intention except to make a demonstration, or may commit a fault. Only, by the same token, as in the defensive the principal end is to be able to act to maintain oneself upon the decisive point, and in the offensive this end must be to execute the most important enterprise, without deranging oneself, a demonstration cannot be harmful.

If the enemy has no other intention save making demonstrations, his movements, on a day of battle, can be separated into those which are achieved in a short space of time and occur in place, or into those which require more time.

Against the first one employs sure reserves, second lines, the method of deploying the troops, or their sending off in columns, their ease and speed in forming up, their art in breaking up and forming anew, etc.; to the last one will oppose the movements and maneuvers convenient.

In the offensive, the victory can be decided by that situation alone when one will have pushed the attack with the greatest activity to end it as soon as possible, and to put oneself also in a state of taking in very little time some dispositions against all the movements which the adversary can make.

In the defensive, on the contrary, it is necessary, depending upon circumstances, either to let the enemy advance, who misses the true point of attack, for falling upon his flanks or upon his rear, or to advance oneself rapidly with the bulk of one's forces to take advantage of the fault that the enemy commits in not employing against our forces but a weak part of his own; when he splits his troops, in attacking one sector, changing our position, and in case of fatuous circumstances, abandoning them entirely, is what one can always do, even in the enemy's presence, when he has thoughtlessly directed his attack, etc.

Circumstances alone can determine the resolution which it is necessary to take. The principles of tactics are very well-known; but the art of applying them appropriately characterizes great generals.

3. Of Partisan Corps

Partisan corps have as their end the misleading of the enemy, of worrying him, of forcing him to make detachments, in a word, doing in miniature what demonstrations do on a large scale.

They are in this regard very useful, and should be frequently employed when the circumstances, the reciprocal position of the two armies, a numerous light cavalry or very superior, and the nature of the terrain permit.

To be efficacious they must, except in entirely open country, consist of weak detachments of light cavalry, because these detachments slide through everything, escaping the vigilance of the enemy, and by this succeed with very little difficulty in everything where one judges it appropriate to employ them; because they find in all surroundings means of going farther and of seeing to their subsistence, and because at worst the loss of such a detachment will have almost no influence upon the effectiveness of the army.

Above all one utilizes partisans to worry the communications of the enemy, to menace his magazines, destroy or carry off his convoys, force him also to cover, by important detachments of troops, his depots and his transport, or for constraining him, by some incursions into the countries which he has weakly occupied, to detach there portions of his army.

The leader of a partisan corps should never forget that he is destined to lead the enemy into error; he will thus avoid all which can give to his adversary the possibility of judging his intention and his force.

He will be *indefatigable,* because he will be discovered soon enough if he stays a long time in one country at the same point, or if he pursues a constant direction in his march; he will be *clever,* to mislead the enemy by his conduct, by his movements, by the divulging of wrong noises and false news, by some publications. by all imaginable ruses; he will be *resolute,* not to let escape a favorable occasion of executing a good blow. and to put that occasion to profit as promptly as possible.

Who can, to use a more just title, be more bold than a partisan in a decisive instant, as well as accompanied by an easy prudence, when he reflects upon the utility for the army that he will have, at the same time as in case of failure he is exposed at worst, and always, to causing the loss of his weak detachments?

4. On War Against the Turks

The Turks have their special manner of making war, because their national character, their religion, their form of government, their customs, make them entirely different from other European nations.

The Turk has a strongly constituted body: he is courageous and bold, and possesses a particular ability in the handling of his own arms.

The horses of the Turkish cavalry are good; they possess a particular agility and rapidity. But their armies totally lack the auxiliary sciences and all that personal bravery cannot replace.

In attacking as in defending, the Turkish soldier, considered in isolation, does more than one could expect from any other; but as the effort of several Turks acts neither to the same end, nor in the same manner, they always fail against an enemy who opposes against them a united mass acting cohesively.

The attack is the most dangerous arm of the Turks; they make them with temerity, with rapidity, in mixed groups of all types of troops, and each isolated man abandons himself to the sentiment of his force. But when such an attack does not succeed, then the feeling of powerlessness acts anew upon those large men who ignore obedience and have not learned, by exercise and practice, to form themselves, to keep themselves in order, to deploy themselves, and they rout with the same disorder and the same rapidity as they came up. That ignorance also renders the Turkish armies incapable of awaiting an attack, of deploying themselves appropriately, or of defending a position.

Here is the manner in which the principles of the art of war should be applied and employed in a war against the Turks.

As the Turks only have advantages in the attack, they will not wait for one to attack them, but always begin by attacking, for constraining, as much as possible, the enemy to the defensive.

The Turk in isolation is bold, rapid and agile. One should thus avoid all combat where the troops, disseminated in small groups, should nearly combat man to man, and to arrange oneself and move in closed bodies, so that the action of several men juxtaposed can easily repulse the efforts of isolated men.

The attacking masses of Turks are formed of cavalry and infantry. The suppleness and rapidity of their horses permit their cavalry to profit from all openings in front or in flank to penetrate there. To give them no chance of doing it, one should thus form the infantry in square, that is to say in the manner where it presents to all sides a closed front, and not to put into lines anything save the cavalry which is equally rapid as their cavalry.

The necessity of opposing to Turks bodies of closed troops is known throughout the world; but the progress of the military art in modem times has brought a difference in the manner of forming them.

The rapidity of the Turks. the slowness of maneuver and the immobility of Christian armies, placed the latter in the impossibility of forming into square upon the field of battle rapidly enough before being prevented in this by the Turks.

They were thus forced to camp and march always in squares, and could not in consequence maneuver in presence of the enemy, because all movements a little long, all passages of a defile, are impossible in square, without breaking it and reforming the troops. They admitted by this the principle of waiting for the Turks with set feet, and looked to augment the difficulty of the approach to their front by fortifying it with *chevaux-de-frises* put in front and by ranging the whole army in a single square, and in forming barricades of wagons; they renounced, in a word, all mobility in presence of the enemy, and looked by all possible means to diminish the force of his attack, something that by which they made all maneuver impossible.

Of all these principles, we have uniquely conserved square configurations for deploying and employing our troops against the Turks.

But as we have adopted as first principle to anticipate the enemy in the attack, which makes necessary prompt and rapid movements, inexecutable with great squares, one is prevented from the formation of the whole army into a single square, and instead today one forms several squares, each one of two or three battalions at most strong. These squares constitute lines of battle as much in march as in position. One forms in the end some of these squares in checkerboard fashion, and from it one derives the great benefit of their being able to mutually defend and support each other.

The mobility of our troops gives us, for all formation and breaking formation, even in the proximity of the enemy, less danger than was had in prior times, above all with small squares, and even if the enemy breaks one, he will have gained little, whereas on the contrary all will be lost if he penetrates into the square formed by the whole army.

It is necessary to send back the cavalry as reserve behind the wings of the squares and their intervals, not as before for awaiting the enemy with firm stance, but for supporting the infantry, and assailing the enemy if he approaches too close, or is ready to be taken.

A barricade of wagons before the army presents the same inconveniences as when the army forms itself in square. That barricade, that *chevaux-de-frise,* briefly, all which can hinder mobility, is as dangerous in a war against the Turks as in all others.

Only a prudent general will send back and arrange his baggage and parks in several barricades of wagons following the same principles which serve them to form and to send off their infantry in squares, as soon as he will be in the proximity of the enemy, and these baggages and parks find themselves exposed to the movements and the attacks of the adversary.

In the war against the Turks the emplacement of outposts merits a special attention. All troops which form the outposts will be sent out in several fractions, and have to fight in an isolated fashion until the first attack of the enemy. With the rapidity of the Turks, and the advantages which they procure from their manner of combat, the outposts have to be not only very attentive, but they should neither be pushed too far, nor be too exposed, without having nearby a troop in closed ranks to receive them. It thus is necessary that the avant-gardes be strong and in part composed of troops of the line, or even that they be placed so near the army, that the van can be promptly supported by that same army.

5. Changes Produced in the Manner of Conducting War by the Last French Wars [1808]

The principal changes in the way of conducting war produced by the recently terminated French wars, are founded on a much greater mobility of troops, and by this of armies, a mobility brought about in part by necessity, and on the other hand by the national character of the French people.

The war of the Revolution broke suddenly, without the necessary preparations for the organization and the subsistence of the armies: it resulted in a system of requisitions as much on French soil as in foreign lands, and from this system arose the possibility of more prompt, more rapid, unlooked-for movements, because it was no longer necessary to have such important magazines, and that the convoys of provisions that swept behind an army in each of its movements could be diminished.

The French armies were hastily composed of peasants recruited from the countryside. The most difficult of soldierly formations, the habit of staying in close ranks, could not be inculcated into them in the small amount of time they had disposable; they thus used the advantage of their natural character which is audacious, impressionable, light, and they made them fight scattered.

This modification of the military art originally came from a necessity; they organized them in the following campaigns, and they formed from this a system which, by the rapidity of all its movements, gave the French armies a decisive superiority over all others: that is why these last have also adopted it.

It resulted in rapidly succeeding marches one after the other, and by this came the influence of stretched¬out movements of the enemy on the tactics of armies and the combination of maneuvers at great distances, which until then was still unknown.

The greatest mobility of troops, joined to their manner of fightingscattered, also modified the art of positions and augmented the difficulties of defensive war; as those countries which, following the prior formation and manner of combat armies, being inaccessible and impenetrable, and which by this could serve as supports for wings or not be occupied at all, no longer presented any obstacle, and could be traversed not only by some isolated troops, but also by a whole army corps.

This modification produced in many men the opinion of never believing themselves secure save if, masters of the terrain, they have distributed their troops on every point, at the same time as others, declared enemies of all innovation, blame the least dissemination of their troops during a combat as harmful and not conforming to the end.

Reflection, as well as experiences, should always confirm, more and more, all military men in the principle of never scattering their forces where they can act in a decisive manner, and prove to them the necessity of conserving their united troops to be able to maneuver; if they keep in effect their troops united upon the decisive point, even a superior number of enemies that skirmish scattered around them, could not give them a serious advantage, but these enemies carry even the danger of being broken if he has need by throwing himself with all his forces upon that portion of their troops which are the most menacing in his estimation, and to be content with amusing the rest only; because, if he calculates his attack carefully, all the other detachments of the enemy will come too late to the aid of the attacked detachments, and while that detachment is going to be precisely attacked, they can undertake nothing decisive for delivering it or disengaging it.

On the other hand, if one takes counsel of experience as well as knowledge of the human heart, one will admit to oneself that rarely, even after a long war, one finds an irreproachable countenance in a troop that stays closed, during which enemy sharpshooters let fly around it, worry it with fire, and kill several men of it in front.

A line so exposed to fire of sharpshooters will soon enough separate from itself, either to march in disorder upon the adversary in the hope of defending itself by this means and pushing them from it, or for saving itself; and thus is not the enemy sure of victory, when he has behind his sharpshooters a reserve body that advances in closed column?

As it is necessary to oppose the same arm to an enemy who deploys skirmishers, it is only necessary in that regard to determine the exact measure of force of the detachments that one should employ as sharpshooters; but it is necessary not to lose sight of the principle that one should only detach as sharpshooters a weak part of one's troops, and always conserve the far stronger part in closed reserve for striking the decisive blows. The determination of this proportion depends upon the force and type of one's troops, as well as that of the enemy's troops, of the terrain on which one fights, etc., in a word, on the situation in which one finds oneself.

Sharpshooters should do in miniature what avant-gardes and rear guards do normally. They should occupy the enemy, fatigue him, discountenance him, keep his sharpshooters away reconnoiter the enemy position and its approaches; in a word, in attacking as in defending, a prudent general will employ sharpshooters to act before the decisive combat, for preparing, if one pardons the expression, the impression which will be produced by the apparition or the fire of the closed troops; but it will always be with closed troops that he will strike the decisive blow.

6. Conclusion

The principles of military science have been, are, and will always be the same, because they are based upon incontestable mathematical truths. Also, they are few in number, because there exist few such truths.

The first of all these principles reposes upon the necessity of an exact calculation of the means to employ for attaining the end, because it is an irrefutable truth that one can never effectuate anything without employing for it sufficient means. These means are the forces. They could be very numerous or small in number, and of this or that type, but they must always suffice to correspond to the intention.

There is for each force a time during which it produces its maximum effect, and when this is come, it should behave and use itself finally entirely for its proper task.

At the epochs of their greatest effect one can promise oneself the most decisive results. The general should thus know how to determine that point with justice, to establish the calculation of the times, foresee the results, because the surest means of conquering is the exact determination of the instant at which the greatest mass of his own forces can attain the highest degree of efficacy.

Another mathematical truth teaches us that it is not necessary to attend any result, when the opposing forces are entirely equal. Thus for the power of promising oneself a favorable result, it is necessary to have or to know how to create artificially a superiority of forces, either by the number or quality of the troops, or by the talent of the general, or by the nature of the terrain, etc., differentiating from these the employment of the same principle of refusing one wing and concentrating their forces on the other.

As the forces are worn out themselves by their own efforts, it is necessary to restore them when they must continue to operate, to act. From that comes the decisive necessity of always covering one's lines of communications and the impossibility of a solid and durable operation whenever ones separates oneself from them.

Why finally is there always a decisive point? Because it is not natural that several points will be identically similar in everything, and that following this one cannot attain the greatest result in the most certain way save upon a single point.

The principles of military science are few and invariable, but their application never resembles them and can never resemble them.

Each change in the reciprocal proportion of the armies, in their arms, their forces, their position, each new invention necessitates a different application of these principles and how can one imagine in human life, and above all in war, a case that is found similar in every respect to a past event?

Epaminondas and Frederick of Prussia both gained victories by the oblique order, but how different between them the employment of the same principle of refusing one wing and of concentrating their forces on the other wing.

The Greeks fought in closed ranks, their arms only reached short distances; ergo, the attacking wing of Epaminondas formed a solid mass.

In our days, where artillery acts so energetically and at such great distances, the attack cannot take place save in several non-closed lines.

The mass formed by Epaminondas presented almost as much depth as width; it marched freely, without fearing outflanking of a wing, because it could face front everywhere. How could that be possible with a corps to which one cannot give, because of the powerful effects of artillery, more than three men of depth, and within danger of seeing the whole line battered in enfilade by the fire of enemy artillery, should one expose his flanks in some way.

To merit the title of general, it is not enough to be familiar with the principles of military science, it is also necessary to know how to apply them. The study of tactical books alone thus will not suffice, because the cases presenting themselves are so numerous and so different that it is impossible to give determining rules for everything.

That art of application cannot be obtained save by the learning of the history of wars, by the meditation and the appreciation of past events, when one will be given some intelligence of the thing and some *coup d'oeil* by a frequent practice upon the terrain. In a word, to become a general, it is necessary to form him oneself.

—The end of *Gründsaetze Der Höhenkriegskünst*, published 1808

Figure 4. Archduke Charles at Aspern-Essling
(painting by Johann Peter Krafft).[3]

---

[3] http://commons.wikimedia.org/wiki/File:Johann_Peter_Krafft_003.jpg

TRANSLATOR'S NOTES

By 1806, when this work was commissioned, the Austrian army had just experienced its worst catastrophe ever in military terms in the campaigns of Ulm and Austerlitz. To renew confidence amongst both officers and men, the Kaiser's brother Charles—the sole general of the army who had had a record of success against the French— was appointed to chair a committee to redefine tactical and strategical procedures to restore some unity of thought and cohesion in action to the operations of the demoralized army, which by that point was factionalized almost to the point of internecine warfare.

Austria had benefitted from such undertakings before, ever since Montecuccuoli's *Sulle Battaglia* came out after the Thirty Years War in like fashion. Similar efforts, though not always crowned by written summations like Montecuccuoli's or Charles', occurred under Prince Eugene of Savoy after the wars of Louis XIV, and by Traun after the War of the Pragmatic Sanction or Austrian Succession and by that of Lacy after the Seven Years War which ended in the acceptance of the cordon system. This system as properly practiced was no different than any other system as far as effectiveness, having its good and bad points as all do; but by the time of the French Revolutionary and Napoleonic Wars it had degenerated until only the shell of the system remained. Properly utilized, it made use of extensive fieldworks to strengthen the outposts of the army, reinforceable by localized reserves, and finally assisted at need by a final reserve for the army.

This allowed large areas of countryside to be covered by the small professional armies of the late Ancien Regime and often resulted in so much artificial strengthening of the outpost line that the opposing army was unwilling to risk attacking it and wasting that expensive commodity, the trained soldier. But the French Revolution changed all that by introducing an enemy that suddenly was willing to accept such heretofore unacceptable losses. To compensate, the cordon system began to take steps, of which the simplest was the strengthening the outpost line by greater portions of the reserves—though this resulted in more victories on the line, it meant that where a breakthrough did occur, less was available to deal with it, and so it became more severe in its effects. The Cordonists, however, maintained that the years of success under the system were too many to discard lightly that system, as proposed a growing number of younger officers led by the Archduke Charles— who were what one might call "Concentrationists." This group felt that only by uniting the bulk of the army and by concentrating all tactical effort on a single point would more success be achieved— and Charles' campaigns seemed to prove it. He had a phenomenally good one in 1796-7 against Moreau and Jourdan, an adequately successful one in 1799—though his withdrawal to the Rhine frontier allowed Masséna to defeat Suvarov—and a fairly good one in Italy in 1805, where he bloodied Massena's nose at the Caldiero. He had only once

73

met Bonaparte in the wars, at the very end of the Italian campaign, where he managed to avoid the traps laid by Masséna and Bernadotte—directed by Napoleon— and helped get Austria off with the Peace of Leoben.

During this time he had lost some minor affairs, one small fortress (Gradisca) and one rather large engagement at the crossing of the Tagliamento,; that, however, was a rearguard action and had been expected to be followed by a retirement in any case. The final setting of the Cordonists' sun occurred in the 1805 campaign, where, at Ulm, the combinations of Mack—a staff college analyst and adherent to this theory —led to disaster.

As a result, post-war Charles was named "Generalissimo" of the Austrian armed forces and strove to reform in his image all the myriad aspects of that military system. This booklet, *Gründsätze de höhen Kriegskünst für die Generale der Österreichischen Armee* (literally, Principles of High Warcraft for the Generals of the Austrian Army;, *Principles of War,* for short) was intended to bring that about. It was intended as a "primer" in generalship, a basic work to be of use to a particularly diverse readership, written to achieve an elementary ordering of their thought and actions; in short, "getting everyone on the same wavelength."

It did not reveal the *only* way to do things. It was not necessarily the *best* way of doing things. But its printing secured for the Austrian army that minimum of cohesion needed to explain the post-1806 campaigns from those before—a difference between respectable conduct and conduct rather worse. It became thus the *Austrian* way of doing things, and rejuvenated a system so it once more could hold its head high amongst the other military traditions of the world. Yet within it lay the seeds to prevent its maker from obtaining full use of it for the Archduke fought but one campaign with his little book before his forcible retirement. *Principles of War* had great popularity thereafter—a British general, Sir Charles Napier[4], wrote to his brother that he found it of more use for his battles in India and Burma than Napoleon's soi-disant *Maxims,* Lloyd's work, Guibert's, or the information his own brother gave regarding Wellington on the Peninsula.[5] Yet this is the first English translation.

Archduke Charles did have an earlier work of his translated into English which was a memoir called Principles of Strategy and dealt with his 1796-7 and 1799 campaigns; it was first put into French by Jomini to go along with his history of the wars of the French Revolution, which in the Jomini-mad pre-American Civil War era became duly translated into English. This was his history of the 1796 campaign against Moreau and Jourdan. One other work, on the 1799 campaign, is yet to come out in this tongue. The *Principles* have also been translated into Italian and Latin.

---

[4] His was likely the best one word telegraph in military history—at the siege of Sind, he wrote "Peccavi", [Latin for "I have sinned"]—until it was, perhaps, superseded by MacAuliffe's "Nuts" at Bastogne a century later.

[5] *A History of the Peninsular War* by William Napier.

The *Principles* were speedily circulated around Europe after their first printing, and a copy found its way into the hands of the prolific Prussian writer von Muffling, whose campaign histories written under his alias/pen name of "C de W" flooded the market in the twenty years after 1806. Muffling wrote some commentaries on the work which no doubt would be of interest if they were easily obtainable—despite extensive efforts and assistance from many students of Napoleonic history, this translator has not been able to get a copy of these comments.

Before examining the *Principles* too harshly, it must be understood that the actual original and the first translations had explanatory diagrams on plates to illustrate Charles' points in a practical manner. These have not as yet been reproducible for reprints and later translations in a fiscally acceptable manner (i.e., it costs too much). Viewing these is of critical interest to the serious in depth researcher, so these must search out an original or early translation for them. One French translation copy with lithographed and onion-skin overlaid plates is held at the New York Public Library 43rd street annex.

Specific Notes

Tr. Notes on Chapter 1, section 1

This section corresponds well with late 18th century and Enlightenment theory regarding conflict, which Charles uses to justify his position for seeking a decision by combat as soon as possible; something that is alien to that era's methodology. The hand of tradition can however still be seen in the *Ancien Regime* tradition of the soldier as an asset (and a highly expensive one at that) of the state by the cautionary words of the statements that encourage waiting for an "optimal" rather than an "adequate" solution. As such an asset, it (the soldier) was not to be "wasted" without maximum effect—a chilly concern, but better than none at all.

This *weltanschaaung* led to the prevalence of the "bloodless" siege being undertaken in preference to the "bloody" battle, despite the casualties being greater overall from siege operations. The people of the 1700's cannot be blamed for this though, as the mathematical underpinnings of statistics had only just been uncovered by the sage Blaise Pascal, and were of course being first applied to more important things such as calculating gambling chances for card games.

A crucial aspect to be gleaned from this is the emphasis on "one decisive point"—which is a good example of a pendulum swing in theory. Charles' concept of the decisive point is stressed to make an emphasis, to bring everyone to the benefits sought by the clique of the concentrationist camp, and avoiding the perceived error of the cordonists of "in trying to defend everywhere they defend nowhere." But to do so he comes up with as awkward a theory as his opponents! In common with a more modern theory. that of the "Indirect Approach" of Sir Basil Liddell-Hart of Britain, the concept of the "single decisive point" is a part of a logical "loop-system" (in computerese), or to those with less impractical mind bents, what is called a "circular argument."

How does one tell if either of these succeeds when the mental chain is so constrained as to use the path:

"Only Theory 'X' leads to success; ergo if success results, Theory 'X' has been used" and then "If Theory 'X' leads to success; ergo, success results only when Theory 'X' is used" and all the myriad permutations of the same nonsense. The concept of the single decisive point is actually that of there being perhaps a single "best" point which can lead to a decision, but there may be - and likely are - other points that in their cumulative weight for whatever reason outweigh that one in importance, or the action of the opponent may have chosen another equally valid "decisive point" affecting *your* side while *you* have been selecting the most decisive point affecting *his*—and then it is a toss-up, even playing according to the rules of "victory-by-decisive-points"—which may or may not be a valid presumption.

Conflict, and any form of competition, is a two-sided affair. To have it, the foe as well as oneself has to have the will to enter it, and what impels him to keep on with it, a side can only "guesstimate" using its own frames of reference, which may or may not be those of the opponent. The only certain parameters are those of the limitations of the human experience—the mind, the emotions, the soul—with culture being a reasonable fence of probability around the likely possibilities.

Some examples of where the "decisive point" theory fails are --at the battle of Cannae—where the Roman choice of a single decissive point, the Carthaginian center, despite its being actually achieved at the point of failure, did not succeed when opposed to the victorious flank and wing assaults of Hannibal. Or the first Battle of Bull Run/Manassas in the US Civil War, when both sides *knew* that the decisive point was the enemy left flank—that being the closest to the enemy's lines of communication to cut him off from them and the best—i.e. most perpendicular to their own (though here a mutual misconception as to these lines' existence and direction existed). By the theory of the "decisive point" it must be that of the Union right/Confederate left, which as the Union perceived it to be so should have meant that the Union should have won it rather than the fatuous Rebels. Tell that to McDowell; it might comfort his shade. But the only way to distill such is from an ex post facto analysis which has nothing to do with utilizable pre-battle information and how to avoid the situation in the first place!

Ergo, the concept is useless save as a false justification for "Monday morning quarterbacking" as a precognitive tool. Its great benefit, though, as has been said, lay in that during the sweep of the pendulum to the opposite extremity seen by the US Civil War's early results; the perihelion of the plumb would occur in the desirable "middle ground" where both extreme tendencies might abate the other to an endurable level. The assertion of there being "only one point" where a superiority of force can be attained is also an error as it is based upon a mutual evenness of spread of the enemy and a like acceptance of a "single point" theory.

Even given a spread-out enemy, there is as has been shown no real guarantee that the "single point" theory is equally espoused by the foe—in fact, Napoleon preferred to keep several options open at all times. He did so by keeping very strong reserves, which the Austrians with their still-extant concern for optimal utilization of manpower tried to implement by having troops posted as efficiently as possible rather than as was most necessary to win. The state-of-the-art Austrian tactical formation was the double line of troops, by the component battalions in deploted single rank lines or operational lines of unitsin the division mass or battalion mass, with horse on the wings, and a reserve_normally centrally located— for ease of reach. Thus the greatest coverage of front accrued, thus the best utilization of infantry firepower presumptively occurred, and artillery was given its freest field of fire—and regularly it got beaten by enemy forces that were used ostensibly non-optimally.

This caused a strain in the high command that is akin to the miasma of heresy to an ossified hierarchy when its heretical practitioners appear to make miracles. The comment of the Austrian generals that "Bonaparte was not a good general" was founded in fact; he *was* "ignorant of the science of war"—the precise mathematical calculations and the chess moves predicated upon them alone. He adhered to the art, which, like in the art of painting (back in the days when painting still required some art) needs to alter the mathematical truism to arrive at the visual perspective, or aural were the art music rather than painting. Perspective foreshortening, harmonic background—these could not be mathematically inspired. The two-line tactical formation may be altered by the presence of an avant- or rear guard, it may be broken up as Charles later suggests into an echelon formation which can allow for greater concentrations or thinnings of a line, but this remains as the basic formation this elementary work is based upon.

Tr. Notes On Chapter 1 section 2

In this section Charles describes the troop types which are the "building blocks" of the army. This is of importance as it shows the unusual, peculiarly Austrian viewpoints regarding them. Light troops, which elsewhere are considered elite troops, here are relegated to second-class status—yet Austria always had massive numbers of light troops—more than any other power until France in the French revolution. But this was a relict from the days when the Usars, the Croats, the Wallachians (e.g. Austria's emergency levies and peripheral hirelings) and the Insurrectio came only into play after the main armies had been beaten, which meant that their trained core was at a premium as it took so long to replace, while the irregular forces proved unreliable in head-to-head open-field combat.

Austria thus tended to glorify the line troops over all others. Only a few of her best soldiers were culled from these regiments to form grenadiers—no Guards (save a decorative Lifeguard horse unit for palaces of no more than a weak squadron's size—and which supposedly never saw battle) existed, and only the best shots were allowed out of the lines as *jagers*. Ergo the Austrian line battalion line infantry company usually had better individual soldiers to form as a core than did any other power—especially the French who during the Napoleonic period gradually culled all major deviations from an average from her line units, a pattern which parallels the decline in the achievements of the individual units which so stunned the world under the Grande Arrnee. The famous six-company French battalion never saw combat against the foes of the Grande Arméee in its most glorious era from 1805-7—and the tough nine- or eight- company French battalion was never encountered by Wellington's British. Only the rump of I Corps at Talavera—which nearly won over superior British strength—in its new six-company configuration was ever encountered from the Channel/North Sea coast camps' corps of 1803-5 by the Sepoy General. When later this same force was crushed at Bidassoa, it was even less its old self.

Austria's tradition emphasized the "large-unit" theory of tactics - that the victory went to the "big battalions" that could absorb much punishment and be better handled due to being few in number. Another aspect of this was that it reduced the number of potential inept or even inimical subcommanders in the faction-ridden KUK (*Kaiser-und-König*) army. The means of officer selection actually hurt Austria due to the plethora of avenues for reaching high command. Birth, purchase, favor, faction, seniority and even merit all could lead theoretically to high command—and did—though usually some amalgamation of them all was required.

Thus one could never be sure why another was placed over oneself. Take "The Unfortunate Mack" for example. Born a poor, non-noble Protestant townsman, was he elevated to the post of éminence grise for Archduke Ferdinand d'Este by his merit? (For he had come up with the first foiling of the French skirmishing tactics by ordering Colberg's men to assume "open order") Or was it for his seniority as a commanding general? (He had after all been commander-in-chief of the entire forces of a state—true, Bourbon Neapolitans—but still, commander-in-chief)? Or was it from his toadying to Thugut, the Prime Minister? Or was it from his prominence as a reforming Cordonist theoretician? Or was it because of his humble birth, which meant he was less likely to embarrass the *Hofkriegsrath* or the Cabinet with noble-egotistic independence and be less likely to spring a coup than another with close family connections? None under him knew.

As for Ferdinand d'Este, only an Archduke by marriage and not birth, whence came his just right of command? From the coffers of the crown still agleam with Ferraran gold from his sister's dowry? From his mere courtly rank socially as

Archduke? From actual combat merit? From his being a Concentrationist like his young brother-in-law? Though such command arrangements might work—and even work out, well if things would only go well—in the actual event, when things began falling out of place and two theoretical abstractions of "optimum" military theory held captive in stupor the men both purported to wish to save, as their French opponent would not be choosing a "best" strategy, it was a demoralizing doom to say the least. Et voilà Ulm!

The *Principles* was, as has been said, basically a primer, an elementary basic reference of the "fundamentals" of Austrian military art, so its exaggerations for effect should not be taken too seriously. Ergo, it did not mean that the only time light horse could ever be used was outside of regular combat as might be implied here.

One specific thing to note is that when Charles refers to "light" artillery, he refers to what would be the Austrian *Kavallerie* battery - a horse artillery-like unit which would be used as specified here, not as a battery solely to support horse but to act in the manner wherever placed. The *Kavallerie* part came not from a necessary association with the cavalry, but from the fact that its cannoneers were mounted atop the (horse-drawn) "wurstwagen" ammunition limbers and wagons, The Austrians meanwhile were getting rid of the regimental cannon that accompanied the line infantry and forming them into *Brigaden* batteries—which came about from their perceived task, which was to "accompany" (i.e., "brigade with") the infantry lines in their tasks —in essence performing their same task as they had done as regimental guns, only now being used in massed numbers for more decisive effect (cf. Chapter II, section III, below). If it seems confusing to the reader, it was just as confusing to the Austrian officers who, from the use of these terms, mixed them up with other powers' terminology (many soldiers drifted from service to service in those days) and got the idea that *Brigaden* batteries could only be attached to a certain brigade, or *Kavallerie* batteries could only be assigned to cavalry units, or that position batteries could only be set up at the beginning of a battle and not move, or any other of the various permutations of lack of sense that ensue when human beings are asked to rely on the written word rather than common sense.

Given the demoralized state of the Austrian army; more and more, as things looked bleaker, they would be turning to such a book to get themselves out of situations, and the Archduke's own caveat about this course of action was regrettably placed at the end of the book, which few would review in the heat of action. Thus in the first campaign after the issuance of the book the Austrian artillery suffered a drop in its efficiency (cf. Major Samek's work on this). Austrian artillery as a whole had a major difference from every other country's. When the French artillery expert Jean-Baptiste Vaquette de Gribeauval, (1715-1789) went off to study under the cannon casters of the *KUK*, he observed that their efforts were focused on strengthening the metal so that they could make lighter pieces, due to the circumstance that in no matter which direction Austria might fight, there was *bound* to be *at least one* mountain range to cross!

Austria solved this problem by those structural *improvements and* by physically shortening the gun muzzle by $1/3^{rd}$ from the standard of other countries. Gribeauval, on the other hand, reasoning that as most of France's wars were in the flatter areas of Flanders and the Palatinate, *increased* the muzzle length by the same distance—$1/3^{rd}$ of the standard of the prior days. This resulted in a muzzle length difference.. This had a bearing on the range and accuracy of the respective shots—the Austrians in fact having what passed for a "land carronade." This difference was not directly proportional, but it was significant. Further, the Austrians stuck to the doubling system of increments in the base 12 system of 3, 6, and 12-pounders, while the French went to evenly-spaced increments of 4, 8, and 12. Though the French later went to the 6 and 12 system (the soi-disant An IX system), the bulk of Gribeauval's other changes remained.

So much for the oddities of the "building blocks" Austria and Charles had to use. One thing that cannot be addressed enough, however, is the dichotomy between the view of the light and line troops here and vis-à-vis the French, Russians, Prussians, Swedes, and the part of the British who regarded them as elite troops. Surprisingly, Wellington was a "heavy" man who sided more with Charles' view as to the use of lights—at least until the Light Division and Crauford changed his mind. Sir John Moore, however, was a "Lights" man from the beginning—though he in his turn was rather unfair to the line troops. There's always something!

Tr. Notes Chapter 1, section 3

Here we see Charles' second attempt to switch the Austrian mindset from defensive to offensive warfare, again an issue brought the Cordonists into conflict with the Concentrationists. Despite the grudging acceptance of the first paragraph, in which the defeated side managed to get the qualifier "decisive" before "superiority," this section as a whole is oriented to the offensive option. Even when on the defensive the general is reminded that without an offensive, no decision will be reached, and so he must be ready to shift over to that mode of action as soon as the case presents itself. Moreover, unless "inevitably necessary" he *must* wage offensive war.

A corollary to the above would be its inverse: while on the offensive, ever to be alert for any need to shift to the defensive as well. Thus did the French act despite the seeming attack-mindedness of the Imperial philosophy of war, in both strategy and tactics. Austerlitz, it must be recalled, was a fight where two corps of the French stood on the defensive, on a field prepared ahead of time with fieldworks after a weeklong French retreat! The counterstroke that won it was offensive, but the defensive stands by Lannes and Davout made the central stroke of Soult and Bernadotte and Murat possible. Such a corollary was likely ignored in the book due to the possibility of its being used as a "loophole" to revert to the defensive mindset at every opportunity—which, though a trifle simplistic, was how the faction-fevered Concentrationists viewed their Cordonist counterparts (the latter of course having just as short shrift for the dunderhead attack-mad set).

Tr. Notes, Chapter 1, section 4

This again deals with elementary matters; like a sports team faced with a string of losses, Austria's army is here "going back to fundamentals." By this section, the commander is reminded to make plans "to finish quickly" (implying previous experience with overly complex plans based on lengthy preliminary maneuvering—did Weyrother's plan for Austerlitz sit in their minds at this point?— probably); to do so only after *certain* knowledge of the enemy's means and the country in which one will operate (did the ignorance of the advent of I Corps in both 1805 campaigns, and the unfamiliarity with the Moravian terrain near Brünn that proved so decisive at Austerlitz, cause this concern–? probably); and to protect the lines of communication on the offensive as well as on the defensive (is the criticism of Melas' conduct pre-Marengo too muted here?). All these give a picture of an army whose leaders at least felt that they were leading a force prone to go off half-cocked, insouciantly, into intricate evolutions and useless battles. Quite a morale builder. But at least it was being at last openly addressed, not whisperingly gnawing in the backs of everyone's mind.

Tr. Notes, chapter 1, section 5

Here the reader is introduced to Austria's "New Method", which involved stripping all secondary theaters for the benefit of the "primary" or "decisive" one alone. This had been tried in 1805 in a half-hearted way, Austria manfully restraining herself to only two armies rather than the three to four she usually tried to field in the Revolutionary Wars; and one, Charles' own Italian Army, was over twice the size of the other (Mack's). This was due to the anticipation that Bonaparte would throw his first effort into Italy, while in Germany the upstart would rest on the defensive to avoid opening a second front.

Therefore the army posted to the German frontier began small, awaiting the arrival of contingents from the various German states: 20,000 Bavarians, 8,000 Wurttemburgers, 6,000 Hessians from Cassel and Darmstadt, etc., and the arrival of two Russian armies of 40,000 each, which would justify the name of *Hauptarmee* "Main Army", French equivalent - "Grand Armée"), which then would be some one and one-third times as large as Charles, and which then would no longer need to hide behind the cloak of German neutrality. (For that reason the Bavarians and Wurttemburgers and Hessians refused their support—and the first two joined the French!). In 1809 this concept led to the over-concentration in Bohemia which was too unwieldy to shift hastily enough beyond the Danube before the Bavarians and French could concentrate enough to oppose them. By these presents, Austria's finest will move by the shortest path to the enemy, for in that is a decisive battle likeliest. This is interesting as it reflects Charles' confidence in the "mauling"—but not the campaigning—abilities of his troops. For the optimum battle, though eagerly to be sought, must yet be approached cautiously, while the pursuit is what should be pushed along as far as possible. By implication, the opposite faults are to be found in Austria's previous commanders.

Tr. Notes, Chapter 1, section 6

Charles' grievances against the Cordonists surface here; a mistake, for it alienates that faction's adherents. That system, as has been shown, was more apropos to the combat-shy 18th than the bloodthirsty 19th century, but it still had its uses. One of the finest examples of a "Cordon defensive system" was the series of fieldworks called "The Lines of Torres Vedras" that were erected by Wellington in Portugal. Like Daun or Lacy, Wellington kept sufficient uncommitted reserves to give the fieldworks strength and impermeability, which later adherents to that system often forgot to include because the utilization of these men in the line gave them the chance further extending the fieldworks horizontally and to "beef up" the front line itself. Charles points out here the chief advantage of the Concentrationist position in defeating separated army incursions; this is relict from his own heyday, the 1796 campaign, where he so treated both Moreau and Jourdan. The part dealing with mountain warfare likewise came from experience, in Switzerland, the Schwarzwald, and the Alps where this Archduke had fought.

Tr. Notes, Chapter 1, section 7

The statements in paragraphs 8-11 were not in the 1806 version, but were found in the French translation of the work from 1856, and are treated here as being part and parcel of Charles' thought with the rest. These may be interpolations by the translator or be alternately sourced (possibly from some source like Rogniat). But they match the style of Charles' thoughts.

Tr. Notes, Chapter 2, section 1

Here is Charles stressing the benefits of reliance on water transport as did the French, trimming the length of the supply columns again; now only 8-10 days of supplies will be held in the army trains. Finally, fortresses must be supplied over complement to insure a proper siege is required to take them, something that had been neglected in 1806, with most Prussian fortresses along the Baltic and the western frontier of that realm (Stettin, Prenzlau, Erfurt, Spandau, Kustrin, Frankfurt-an-der-Oder, and Magdeburg).

Tr. Notes, Chapter 2, section 2

The advice that "Marches should be scouted, light troops should be located in van and rear guards to do this task" implies that this was not always the case. The admonishment to form as many columns as possible is not, despite popular folklore, something drawn from the Revolutionary (French) Wars experience; it was also part of the cordon system, as that was the only possible mode of advancing the extended lines of their formations. This fact explains the caveat carefully added here regarding the necessity of sufficient strength and the aspect of mutual support. The concept is again "opti-linear"—for the best line possible—and carried with it the unhappy requirement that one must have an exact know-ledge of the location of one's foe (not always feasible). When not known, the weak flanks are liable to "outrage" (an archaic term for being compromised). A key to under-standing Charles and his differences from Napoleon is that Charles subordinated marches to the battle line, while Na-poleon, if anything, subordinated the battle line to marches (a "chicken or the egg" problem).

Tr. Notes, Chapter 2, section 3

The delineation of positions mentioned here might tele-graph one's intentions to a wary foe. Here Charles describes territorially his pet concept of the "decisive point" as being usually either a flank or some exposed salient, which could hinder an assault on the enemy line. The comment regarding cavalry is proper in that for cavalry to utilize properly *l'arme blanche*" or shock tactics, it needed to acquire a certain impe-tus. Were it to be posted along the exact line which it had to hold, it would be receiving any enemy charge at a halt, aban-doning its best assets of maneuver, speed, and surprise. The solution preferred, which states of the importance of this for the *defensive* utilization of horse, would tend even more to reinforce the conservative nature of Austrian cavalry han-dling remarked about by Napoleon in his comments on Lloyd. In this section too springs forth Charles' fascination with the use of echelons. This would have a major effect on the conduct of the second day at Wagram.

Tr. Notes, Chapter 2, section 4

This again refers to the Cordonist habit of entrenching everywhere.

Tr. Notes, Chapter 2, section 5-c

Here too the concentration is on avoidance of errors; troops are to rely either on force or surprise to effectuate passage of river barriers, when attacking, and to remain concentrated behind the river to punish any attempt at crossing when one defended them. This meant a concentration on smiting the leading edge of the column passing over before enough of it had crossed to assure victory. It contrasts with the preference of Napoleon, who wrote Viceroy Eugene that to defend a river line such as the Oder, the best means was to hold one's troops concentrated on the far side of the river to distract the enemy into dealing with them first in order to avoid the possibility of those troops falling on the tail end of the enemy's columns.

Bernadotte, however, took another option, at Spanden in 1807 (and again in 1809 & 1813) where he apparently preferred to be "à cheval"—astride—river lines with a small tête-de-pont (bridgehead) well-entrenched on the far side but occupied by minimal troops, while the bulk of his corps rested behind it on the far side of the river. By this either the enemy would not be concerned with the small protuberance and would ignore it, in which case the bulk would swiftly pass over to smite the enemy tail, or else a battle of attrition would ensue between the occupants of the bridgehead and their attackers, a combat in which all favored the defenders, sheltered by earthworks, fronts swept by unapproachable batteries on the "safe side." Moreover, sufficient reserves existed to reinforce—and even "spell"—the defenders as they wearied.

All three methods could work under confident generals, all three could be pure catastrophes if the plan used for one was applied to another.

At Friedland, Bennigsen assaulted Lannes, who acted in Charles' approved way, and in the second phase of the battle, when Bennigsen had already passed the army over, the Russians were acting as Napoleon advised, making a "far side" *defense* (which worked insofar as it indeed forced the French to attack the Russians on the same bank before passing the stream—though it must be admitted that if such influenced Bennigsen it was not apropos - as the French had had no intent to cross the Alle) in a terrain that only suited for a Bernadottian-style bridgehead defense. There was not enough perimeter or depth to the Russian to allow them to use their forces adequately. The Napoleonic far-side required a position removed from any tactical barrier cramping the rear area and/or transit of reserves.

One of the most misunderstood aspects of Leipzig in 1813 is the way in which the shifting of the French lines of communication to the west via Hof and Frankfurt-am-Main rather than the northeast to the Elbe and Magdeburg-Dresden a) had to be accomplished and b) what effect it had on the battle. But room is here lacking for that tale. Worth noting is the curious fact that of all of the "First Captains" of the Napoleonic era, Wellington never had to deal with the problem of defending a river line—mainly as the terrain of the Peninsula was not amenable to this course, moving parallel to rather than athwart his paths as he penetrated north of the Ebro in 1813. He did pass the Nivelle, which Soult defended in southern France in 1814, but Soult by then was grievously weakened and was relying on an impressive looking series of earthworks for a cordon-style defense to gain what time he could before the Sepoy General found out that it was but a baguette's crust.

Again, the "primer" style of the *Principles* assumes a single, easily identifiable line of operations on the part of the enemy. To the opportunistic French Revolutionary generals, and above all to Napoleon, this was not so easy. In 1809, for example, he could have a) moved south to cut off the Archduke John's army in an Ulm/Jena rerun or a la Marengo, or b) he could have driven North into Bohemia to join the Saxons and Baltic dregs under Bernadotte's Saxon and Poles and Jerome's largely Westphalian armies to secure Bohemia first (which possibility in fact slowed up Charles' army enough that Vienna was lost), or c) he could drive headlong for Vienna (seemingly the least probable or wise of the three options). Later in the campaign, once at Vienna, he could have moved north into Bohemia, or could have driven further along the Danube into Hungary to foment revolt in that perennially restless realm, or he could have driven into Moravia again—this time joining with his Polish allies who had just moved upon Cracow and were spreading into Galicia. The first threat resulted in the absence of V Korps and the second in the absence of Archduke John's "army" (of corps size) for the crucial battle of Wagram.

Tr. Notes, Chapter 2, section 6

This section on "cantonments" has the view that an army that uses them is carrying a mark of inferiority to the enemy - as something to be resorted to only in unfortunate circumstances. It made taking them up a visible admission of incapacity, and thus tended to demoralize the army building them. It posed a severe problem to the main army undertaking their construction in 1809 where it rendered the morale fragile and crystallized the emotional lift brought about by the "victory" of Aspern-Essling.

To combat this it was said at the time by the Archduke that the *KUK* Army would recover the capital "à la Washington" (referring to his camp at Valley Forge in 1777-8). The differences were severe; for one thing, the American encampment was much more distant from Philadelphia than those along the Russbach were from Vienna, it was bitter winter, and any movement by the British would have been telegraphed long in advance—unlike Bonaparte's six-hour passage of the Danube's final arm for three corps. Other factors, such as the political reasons for the British not to risk their undoubted occupation of the Patriot capital by a chancy combat versus the fieldworks, the hopes they had for the

dissolution of the enemy army by spring, and the professional training the final core of American troops had received in
the last few months at Valley Forge, patently made encampment à la Washington an invalid strategy, but it was
the only remotely similar campaign that cast a cheery light
on the Austrian situation and its imperative requirements.
The most recent Austrian strategic examples were a half-
dozen or so undertakings by the Cordonists, so, rather than
strengthen that faction, a model had to be sought outside the
bounds of the *KUK* service. The contemporary [1809] reference to Valley Forge is worth noting as it antedated by some
one hundred years any other serious examination of US military affairs and campaigns as being applicable to European
conditions until the trench warfare of WWI tended to in-
crease interest in the end of the Civil War campaigns and
battles of Grant, Sherman, Sheridan and Thomas vs. Lee,
Johnston, Early, and Hood.

Tr. Notes, Chapter 3, section 2

Demonstrations are described in a manner that reinforces
the theme of the work: caution, calculation, foresight, awaiting events, and avoiding bungling. The motto of the entire
book is effectively "Don't screw up!"—which by implication
asserts that in the past Austrian leaders had done just that.

Tr. Notes, Chapter 3 section 3

The emphasized personality traits were capitalized in the
French translation, not in the original German edition. This
entire section deals with distant detachments of light troops

into partisan corps ("raiding parties") which were a forte of the *KUK* Army, and foreshadowed the successful partisan operations in 1813-4 by Cossacks and *Freikorps*.

Tr. Notes, Final Chapters

As said, the placement of the chapter on the Turks in greater detail and discussion is evidence, albeit circumstantial, that these were considered the primary future enemies in 1806-7. The chapter on the French merely gives a short explanation of skirmishing tactics' history, how to use them, and how to counter them only in the vaguest generalities.

The concluding chapter is perhaps the most important in the book. It wraps up the philosophy of "The Austrian Way" and provides the loopholes of bowing to circumstances needed in such a work. The one criticism is that perhaps it was rarely read due to its being at the farthest extremity of the book (not unlike this section) The comparison between Frederick the Great and Epaminonidas of Thebes are peculiarly apropos and elegant The concentration of the work "on a few mathematical principles" is no more in error (and no less) than any appreciation resting upon mathematics and models of any sort derived from math principles. They are models, and as such, have the limitations of the perception of their creator. Ergo, they must be imperfect simulations of reality, and error can enter.

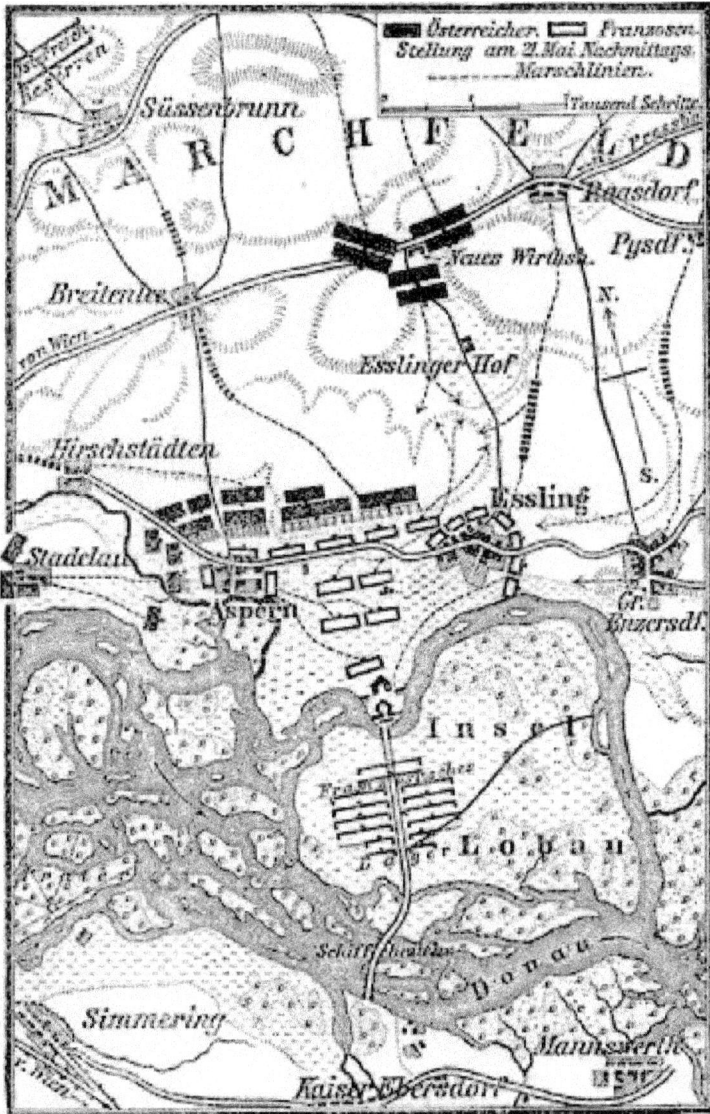

Figure 5. The battle of Aspern-Essling.

Figure 6. The Archduke Charles and his
   children (lithography by Josef Kriehuber,
   1835).[6]

---

[6] http://commons.wikimedia.org/wiki/File:Soehne_des_Erzherzog
_Karl.jpg

www.ingramcontent.com/pod-product-compliance
Lightning Source LLC
Chambersburg PA
CBHW071053090426
42737CB00013B/2343